Developing Civic Engagement in Urban Public Art Programs

Developing Civic Engagement in Urban Public Art Programs

Edited by
Jessica L. DeShazo and Zachary Smith

ROWMAN & LITTLEFIELD
Lanham • Boulder • New York • London

Published by Rowman & Littlefield
A wholly owned subsidiary of The Rowman & Littlefield Publishing Group, Inc.
4501 Forbes Boulevard, Suite 200, Lanham, Maryland 20706
www.rowman.com

Unit A, Whitacre Mews, 26-34 Stannary Street, London SE11 4AB

British Library Cataloguing in Publication Information Available

Library of Congress Cataloging-in-Publication Data

Developing civic engagement in urban public art programs / Edited by Jessica L. DeShazo and Zachary Smith.
    pages cm
 Includes bibliographical references and index.
 ISBN 978-1-4422-5728-3 (cloth : alk. paper) — ISBN 978-1-4422-5729-0 (electronic)
 1. Public art—United States. 2. Artists and community—United States. 3. Community arts projects—United States. 4. Social participation—United States. I. DeShazo, Jessica L., editor. II. Smith, Zachary A. (Zachary Alden), 1953– editor.
 N8844.D48 2015
 701'.030973—dc23

                                                              2015030150

Printed in the United States of America

Contents

Preface

Public art has been an important part of the human condition for some forty thousand years (White 2003, 7). The role and importance of public art has changed over time. Public art had been used for spiritual and religious purposes, for political purposes, and for no other reason than to fill empty space. We believe that a very important role for public art is often overlooked or ignored—sometimes consciously, but most often, we suspect, unconsciously. That role is in the creation of a sense of space and community and belonging. In addition, we believe that at this time in human history it is important to build community and belongingness. Major metropolitan areas in the United States and suburbs all over the world have grown, often with little care of identity—the faceless soulless suburb has become the norm in many sprawling metropolitan cities.

Developing Civic Engagement in Urban Public Art Programs is designed to help arts commissions and public administrators interested in developing public art programs to understand the changing roles of public art and the conditions that are conducive to creating public art that builds community.

In this process, society has become fragmented—people have become disconnected from their location and what they have in common with their community. Robert Putnam was one of the first to popularize the notion that the "civic society has shrunk" and that fewer and fewer people are engaged with their communities, their governments, or their surroundings. This trend is unfortunate, for as Putnam notes: "For a variety of reasons, life is easier in a community blessed with a substantial stock of social capital. In the first place, networks of civic engagement foster sturdy norms of generalized reciprocity and encourage the emergence of social trust. Such networks facilitate coordination and communication, amplify reputations, and thus allow dilemmas of collective action to be resolved" (Putnam

1995, 2). In addition, there is strong evidence that civic and community engagement can play an important role in human mental health (Walsh 2011, 579).

What can public art do for a community? How can city governments and others who create public art develop projects that build community and engage civil
society? That is what this unique collection of chapters address. Public art can build
community unity, identity and cohesiveness.

A primary purpose of this book is to show how cities can engage their citizens
through public art. There are many small- and medium-sized cities that do not
have public art programs. There are how-to books that describe the fundamentals
of establishing a public art program—but there is no work that describes the successes of cities and towns in developing public art in a way that engages and can
transform a community.

Definitions of public art run from the simple to the complex. Scholars of art
have long recognized the importance of the relationship between the art and the
public. As Hilde Hein notes of the modern period: "The audience no longer fig-
ured as passive onlooker but as participant, actively implicated in the constitution
of the work of art" (Hein 1996, 3). But even the most sophisticated descriptions
of public art and its role in society pay scant attention to the role art can play in
civic engagement and the building of community (see, for example, Hein 1996).
It is not uncommon for arts organizations and artists to talk about community engagement: "Today, public art has moved beyond that of permanence and solidity,
seeking to engage the community in a manner that, while not excluding the methods of the past, brings them to life as a part of the community" (Forecast Public
Art). In addition, as the Association for Public Art notes, "public art can express
community values, enhance our environment, transform a landscape, heighten our
awareness, or question our assumptions." The editors of this book could not agree
with these descriptions more but feel these depictions do not go far enough. While
"expressing community values" and "engaging the community" are fundamental to
the best public art, we should also expect more from public art—specifically for it
to build community.

Can public art solve society's ills? Perhaps not, but public art, when well thought
out and placed, can build community and connectedness—and that is an important
start. The chapters in this book recognize this role for public art and in various ways
illuminate the process of creating and managing public art to achieve these ends.

The first part of the book, "The Nature of Public Art and Its Role in Society,"
contains two chapters describing how the role of public art in society and how that
has changed over time.

In chapter 1, "Responding to Site," Anita Glesta explains an artist's process for creating public art. As an artist, she responds to the site by allowing time to familiarize
herself with both the community and the history of a location. She provides readers
with an understanding of how both artists and administrators must work together
to create site responsiveness.

K. M. Williamson's "Public Art in the Hands of the Public Realm," chapter 2 of the book, presents an overview of public responses to public art installations that illustrate forms and degrees of civic engagement with public art. Williamson shows a continuum to demonstrate the intensity of civic engagement ranging from enthusiasm to criticism. Examining the nature of civic engagement with public art illustrates program strengths and weaknesses that can then be addressed with program corrections and policy revisions.

Part II, "Building Public Art That Unites and Defines Communities," offers a look at the efforts of eight cities in creating public art projects or programs.

In chapter 3, Donna Isaac analyzes how a range of funding sources has allowed the Scottsdale Public Art Program flexibility to build both a broad and quality public art pieces. The program has established its reputation for integrating creative place making with community engagement.

In chapter 4, Jean Graham, Carrie Brown, Susan Lamb, and Meghan Wells highlight community involvement for the City of Austin's public art program. They give us an account of how different strategies that are dependent on the specific project may need to be employed to garner community involvement. One must see each project as being unique and cannot take a one-size-fits-all approach.

Robyn Vegas provides us with a sort of blueprint in chapter 5 for those wishing to create or fund public art projects by giving us a tour of the many and varied projects being undertaken in Broward County and the various cities in South Florida.

Mary Allman-Koernig explains how a city can engage businesses in the development and promotion of public art. In chapter 6, she provides useful suggestions for any city wanting to foster the art and business relationship.

In chapter 7, Sherri Brueggemann explains how the Albuquerque Public Art Program has adapted in its thirty-six-year history to internal and external influences.

Dee Hibbert-Jones describes in chapter 8 how the Social Practice Arts Research Center at the University of California at Santa Cruz has engaged in project building between artists, scientists, the public, and others to create public art that brings community together and strives for active social and environmental change.

In chapter 9, Nigel Brookes provides readers with an examination of the players and process involved in the creation of public art projects in the San Diego community of City Heights. This comprehensive case study shows us how many players can come together to create art and fuse community.

Chapter 10 gives an in-depth explanation of how the Los Angeles Department of Cultural Affairs uses the public art process to create civic engagement. Here, Felicia Filer provides a case study that highlights how one can court stakeholders and unite competing communities. In the end, one can create public art that establishes new public gathering and cultural locations.

Preface

REFERENCES

Association for Public Art. Accessed October 4, 2014. http://associationforpublicart.org/public-art-gateway/what-is-public-art/.

Forecast Public Art. Accessed October 4, 2014. http://forecastpublicart.org/toolkit/didactic.html.

Hein, Hilde. 1996. "What Is Public Art?: Time, Place, and Meaning." *Journal of Aesthetics and Art Criticism* 54(1): 1–7.

Putnam, Robert D. 1995. "Bowling Alone: America's Declining Social Capital." *Journal of Democracy* (January): 65–78.

Walsh, Roger. 2011. "Lifestyle and Mental Health." *American Psychologist* 66 (7): 579–92.

White, Randall. 2003. *Prehistoric Art: The Symbolic Journey of Humankind.* New York: Abrams.

I

THE NATURE OF PUBLIC ART AND ITS ROLE IN SOCIETY

1

Responding to Site

Anita Glesta

INTRODUCTION

Creating art for and in public spaces requires timeliness, a strong sense of place, and relevance to the community. These are all aspects of site responsiveness, which I define as sensitivity to the physical nuances of a particular site, its history, and its relationship to the people who use it. Over the course of my twenty years as an artist working in public spaces, I have come to the realization that site responsiveness is the single most important aspect of creating public art. Both artists and art administrators have a responsibility toward the site and its specific needs that can only be fulfilled through our cooperation and mutual understanding. In my experience, artist and administrator cooperation can be improved in numerous specific ways: through the presence of a dedicated artist liaison or project manager; through both pre- and post-installation observation of the site; and through the recognition that compatibility between the artist and site should be a significant aspect of the art administrator's selection criteria. Throughout this chapter, I have drawn on my own successes and challenges to illustrate these ways in which artists and art administrators can work together to facilitate site responsiveness and, ultimately, create meaningful and innovative approaches to public art.

My career as a public artist began in 1994 when I was invited by the Organization of Independent Artists, a now-defunct nonprofit that curated artist exhibitions at public venues in New York City. I was invited to create a temporary public sculpture in the urban parkland that surrounded the Manhattan Psychiatric Center, a mental hospital situated on Ward's Island in New York City's harbor. Up until this point, I had worked almost exclusively as a painter and sculptor, exhibiting in galleries and museums around New York. I knew that the first step in preparing for this work would be to educate myself about the space itself, about the center, and about the people who lived there. In the course of my research, I learned that many of those interned were homeless or indigent. I decided to create an artwork that would reference temporary housing and, through this reference, allude to the interrelated issues of homelessness and mental illness in New York City. I designed two fences of wood resembling a dinosaur's spine rising up from and sinking down toward the ground over a span of forty feet. The fences were made from rows of the wooden planks set at least eighteen inches deep into the ground in order to make them secure and challenging to remove. Finally, I stretched rubber sheeting between these two rows of wood to form a rough tent-like structure.

Two days after the work was installed, I returned to site. To my shock and confusion, I found that about half of the wood planks had been removed. After a quick search, I discovered them in a wooded area of the grounds not too far from the sculpture. They had been recycled into smaller, more inviting, functional shelters and structures that the local homeless were inhabiting.

This unintentional transformation of my work from homage to home was to change the trajectory of my work in the public forever. I found myself questioning my work's intended impact and audience. Could my work really serve the indigent population as a symbolic and referential gesture if I were to restore it to its original sculptural form? To do so felt like an insult in the context of the desperation and need this population faced. After this experience, I was no longer interested in creating works that obtained their meaning and relevance solely through reference. Instead, I decided that my public works needed to engage people directly, either through physical interaction, intellectual engagement, or both. Through this kind of participatory interaction, I realized that my art could offer people a sense of ownership rather than just observation. Creating works that have an interactive component has been central to my work ever since.

While public spaces present almost boundless opportunity for innovation, it is crucial for artists to question our roles and to be engaged in ways that can offer new meaning to a site. If the traditional role of the artist as visionary is to critique society and to illuminate a different view of reality, now is the perfect time to ask ourselves: What can artists do for a particular public space?

This chapter focuses on two recently realized large-scale public projects, each of which illustrates a different answer to this pressing question. The first of these projects, the Census project, is a permanent, integrated landscape/artwork commissioned by the new Federal Census Bureau Headquarters in 2004 and finished in 2010. *GERNIKA/GUERNICA*, on the other hand, was a self-initiated project developed over a course of ten years. It was first installed in 2007 as an outdoor sound sculpture at the Chase Manhattan Plaza in New York City through the Lower Manhattan Cultural Council and a multichannel video installation at White Box Gallery, both nonprofit arts institutions. It has subsequently been shown at numerous museums around the globe. Both projects presented me with unique challenges as an individual artist and as a member of a team of people working together to realize an artistic vision in a public space. In both cases, however, site responsiveness was paramount in my approach.

THE CENSUS PROJECT

The Census project, as a commission from the General Services Administration (GSA), presented the challenge of working on a public site with set boundaries and expectations. I was commissioned to create an artwork spanning the entire seven-acre landscape of the new Federal Census Bureau Headquarters; a 1.5 million square foot building designed by the architecture firm Skidmore, Owings and Merrill to house the Census Bureau's nearly ten thousand employees. When I looked at the original blueprints for the bureau's seven-acre park, I immediately noticed that the design included designated seating for only twenty-five people—hardly sufficient for a workforce of ten thousand. I decided to humanize the space and offer "places" for the ten thousand employees to sit, explore, and enjoy the space. To this end, I designed oversized benches, small seating nooks, and an extensive network of walking paths that form the digits 1 through 8 as one crosses the grounds.

At the same time, I wanted to build a thoughtful, not merely functional, experience. I realized I had the opportunity to create a playful and physically attractive landscape while at the same time offer employees a different way of thinking about and interacting with their work at the Census Bureau. I decided to tackle the concept of "census" physically, through artistic manipulation of landscape and the artist elements embedded within it. Because I work with history and memory, I concentrated on addressing the concept of census through its significance in history.

The census has always been a method of creating and delineating community, ethnicity, and identity. My way of addressing this was not in terms of data but

Figure 1.1.   Census Tile Wall, Federal Census Bureau
Photo by Anita Glesta

through the diverse numerical symbols used throughout history and across the globe. In addition to the more widely known numeric systems of the Arabs, Sumerians, Ethiopians, Mayans, and Persians, I gave special emphasis to Native American systems of counting. I learned that in some of the earliest U.S. Censuses, the Native American peoples gave bundles of twigs to the census takers. Some of the sticks were forked in the end to represent the women; others were small, representing children. I created hand-painted tiles for each of these numerical systems and set them into several landscaped mounds across the grounds. In order to acknowledge those on the margins of personhood, I included tiles painted with fading or emerging figures as a metaphor for the disappeared and the uncounted people of America. These layers of meaning helped transcend the traditional use of numerical symbols, soliciting mythic elements from these usually straightforward signs.

The responses I received from the employees of the Census Bureau were elating. Many employees commented on the Native American numbers, noting that the tiles had made them want to learn more about the original inhabitants of this country. Because the employees work regularly with statistics and numerical data, I received several letters from employees asking whether the numeric symbol tiles represented a game or code that they might figure out! Their level of interaction with my work was far more sophisticated than anything I could have anticipated. When construction issues arose in certain areas of the landscape, one employee contacted me directly to ensure that I was aware of the problem area. In essence, I feel that they have taken ownership of the work and turned it into their own "place."

Figure 1.2.   Census Tile Wall, Federal Census Bureau
Photo by Anita Glesta

The most challenging part of the Census project for me was juggling the dual role of artist and project manager. The GSA did not have anyone in place at the time to represent the artist in the role of project manager, so I was reliant on the construction manager hired by the contractor. While I had hired a landscape architecture firm to do the construction drawings for my design, I could not afford to employ them for project oversight and management work. Essentially, I ended up doing the work of both an artist, developing the concept for the Census project, and the work of an architectural firm, overseeing the minutia of construction and liaising with the client construction manager, contractor, and work crew. On top of this, budget and time constraints meant that I was unable to visit the site regularly to oversee the work during the months of installation. Most communication had to occur over the phone or by email, which often led to miscommunication and compromised the construction process.

Working in this manner was a big learning curve for me and resulted in some problems with the construction quality. In the years since the original installation, I have had to redo a number of the tiles, as the concrete was not properly poured on the walls where they were installed and water has seeped in. The GSA has happily taken responsibility for the problem and has helped to restore the areas that have required rebuilding. With their support, I have recreated the tiles, and a new contractor has been hired to oversee the rebuilding of the concrete walls where there was seepage.

This project taught me just how critical the position of the artist advocate and project manager is in the creation of a large-scale public artwork. Few of us are ever prepared or trained for the enormous complexity that creating art in the public brings, in particular the challenge of working with a large team of people from different fields. It would have made a great deal of difference if the commissioning agent had had a project manager to help oversee the project and facilitate communication between myself and the people working onsite.

GERNIKA/GUERNICA

Unlike the Census project, the concept for *GERNIKA/GUERNICA* preceded the site. In fact, the seeds of the *GERNIKA/GUERNICA* project began in the weeks following 9/11. At the time, I was living only blocks away from the World Trade Center, right at the center of the destruction. I thought about Picasso's great painting *Guernica*, which depicts the effects of the horrific Gernika bombing in 1937, and what it meant to be making art about atrocity, both in general and in the context of a memorial. This correspondence between 9/11 and the Gernika bombing began what became a ten-year project, during which I visited the village of Gernika more than twenty times. I learned that the survivors of the bombing, which killed more than sixteen hundred innocent people and maimed another nine hundred, had never been interviewed before. I recorded their conversations, documented their memories and thoughts about the atrocity, sometimes using Picasso's *Guernica* as a starting point. In juxtaposing Picasso's *Guernica* with oral narratives of the survivors, *GERNIKA/*

8 *Anita Glesta*

GUERNICA formed a dialectical relationship between the way Picasso's painting conceived of the bombing and how the Gernika survivors conceive their own experiences of the day and their lives following it. Disclosing the universal human experiences of tragedy and survival in the wake of loss, as well as the manner in which these issues have been expressed through art history, was the thrust of this work.

The initial public installation of this work was designed specifically for the Chase Manhattan Plaza, which I chose due to its proximity to Ground Zero. I wanted to highlight the relationship between universal memory and specific memorialization by retelling the story of Gernika bombing within a five-minute walk of where the Twin Towers once stood. But beyond simple location, the Chase plaza had its own history to consider. There has always been a large-scale Dubuffet sculpture on one side of the plaza that lends a lyrical abstract and painterly dimension to an otherwise featureless urban space. The population of the sixty-story Chase Manhattan skyscraper, coincidentally also a Skidmore, Owings and Merrill–designed building from the early 1960s, included several thousand people in the finance industry. The plaza is one block away from Wall Street and was a popular lunchtime destination. Creating sculptures that would integrate my vision of *GERNIKA/GUERNICA* smoothly into the physical and demographic environment of the plaza was a challenge.

I saw that there were eight seating areas on the side of the plaza opposite the Dubuffet, where people traversed to enter the Chase Manhattan building and access the subways underneath. I decided that it would offer a dynamic yet subtle intervention if I integrated the sculptures into the seating areas and added the sound dimension through motion activation. This would render an intimate, conversational quality to the work that might invite people to stop and think about their current place in a more historical context through the mediation of an older generation of survivors' narratives.

Figure 1.3.   Census, Federal Census Bureau
Photo by Anita Glesta

On each bench in the plaza, I created a small sculpture resembling a 1930s radio, referencing one interviewee's remembrance of the Gernika bombing. She, like many others, discarded her sacred radio—one of the few points of contact with the outside world available at the time—along with other precious possessions, to flee the bombs. I topped each radio sculpture with bronze body parts, including a human heart, an adult's and a child's hands, a foot, bull's horns, a horse's tail, an oak leaf (a symbol of the village of Gernika), and a small head resembling the head on the bottom left of Picasso's *Guernica*. Into each radio sculpture I placed motion-activated speakers with two-minute narratives of the survivors of the Gernika bombing. When people approached or sat near the small radios on the benches, the movement would prompt stories in Spanish and in English. The radio sculptures were made of iron and waterproof steel encasing outdoor speakers, meant to withstand a lot of human traffic, particularly at lunchtime, when many thousands of Chase employees would sit on the benches to grab a quick bite.

One of the most powerful and transformative features of public art is its ability to reach a wide audience of both purposeful viewers and casual passersby. By using synchronous sources of image and sound, *GERNIKA/GUERNICA* intentionally thrust pedestrians into an assembled virtual reality of both visual and oral history—and this approach was not always received well or as I had expected. I was amazed by the unexpected enthusiasm of local construction workers, who often took the time to circle the plaza and listen to each of the eight boxes. They were not the audience that I had anticipated as being particularly receptive to the work. I was less surprised by the positive response from destination tourists, who heard about the work due to the press surrounding the Lower Manhattan Cultural Council's River-to-River Festival, in which *GERNIKA/GUERNICA* took part. These tourists spent the most significant amount of time engaged with the work.

New York City is a notoriously brutal environment for placing art in the public, but I was happy to see that my work was able to withstand significant use and abuse. Over the course of the four-week installation at the plaza, I visited every two or three days to observe the work's reception as well as oversee the continued operation of the technical components. I saw the "radios" being used as lunchtime trays for Chinese takeout. I saw kids climbing on them as a makeshift jungle gym, and coffee being spilled over the speakers. None of the radios received any damage from this wear and tear. What I had not anticipated were the negative responses, particularly from some of the Chase Manhattan employees. One man even tried to break one of the radio sculptures because the motion-activated narration was interrupting his lunch. I watched him from a distance as he kicked at the speaker. Blog posts sprang up criticizing the work from several different angles. One blogger complained about the noise pollution. Another wrote that the narratives should have been more specifically about the village of Gernika rather than general stories that could have been "anyone's stories"—despite the fact that this universality was the intentional part of my work.

An artist must try to expect the unexpected when creating work for a public site. Nonetheless, I know that I will always be surprised by the final outcome. Instead of considering these bumps in the road as failures, I see them as opportunities for learning and expanding my own perspective and assumptions in response to a site. For this reason, frequent post-installation observation is also a key part of my approach to creating site-responsive, interactive public art. The artist's work does not end with installation.

Visiting a completed artwork not only reveals flaws to be remedied but can also inspire improvements one might otherwise never have considered. After its initial New York iterations, *GERNIKA/GUERNICA* traveled to the Museo de Antropologia in La Paz, Bolivia, and to the Museum of Contemporary Art in Krakow, Poland. In 2013, it inaugurated the new contemporary international gallery of the Arthur M. Sackler Museum in Beijing. At each venue, the work added new translations of the Gernika narratives. Today, survivors' voices can be heard in Spanish, English, Polish, and Mandarin. The Sackler Foundation of the Arts, Sciences and Humanities, which eventually acquired *GERNIKA/GUERNICA*, plans to donate the entire project to the village of Gernika, where it will be placed in a public plaza located in the center of the town. At this final site, the sculptures will include the narratives of the survivors' voices in all the languages, and the work's rich, international legacy will have resonance for a village once bombed for its antifascist identity and now known as a center for peace.

THE ROLE OF PUBLIC ARTIST AND SITE

This is my answer to what public artists can do for a site: artists working in public space can respond to a site in order to enhance and build it into a meaningful "place" by exposing its layers—whether of history, of culture, or of the environment—in subtle and surprising ways. From the artist's perspective, careful research into the site's history, its physical space, and demographics, pre- and post-installation site observation, and successful collaboration with others associated with the project are all essential steps toward the realization of this goal.

This brings me to one final point. In 2011, I designed a public art residency program at the New York School of Visual Arts (SVA) to help professional artists from around the world explore and navigate the complex process of creating art in public space. The "Reconfiguring Site" Public Art Residency Program was structured around my experience as a public artist in New York and internationally. It aimed to give each resident the opportunity to engage with many of the concerns of making art in the public, in particular the challenge of researching and responding to a site.

As is always the case when teaching, I learned alongside my students. Because the residency was short, residents were required to create project proposals in the form of physical or digital maquettes with the accompanying written materials, rather than to realize a complete project. While I encouraged students to site their proposed project in the New York area, one year I was encouraged by the SVA administration to have students design proposals specifically for the newly renovated High Line Park. I could understand the attraction: located only one block from the school,

Figure 1.4. Ward's Island Temporary Installation
Photo by Anita Glesta

the High Line Park was already a popular tourist destination. However, it quickly became apparent to me that the site presented serious obstacles for the novice public artist. The High Line is a relatively narrow, straight space with a highly designed landscape and very few nooks and crannies. To create any kind of physical artistic intervention within the limited context of the site competed with its already near perfect design. Many of my residents struggled, and perhaps the least innovative proposals made during the several years that I taught and directed the program were those developed for this particular site.

What I learned from this teaching experience was that, while it is essential for an artist to consider what he or she can bring to a site, it is also important to ask what a particular site can contribute to the artist or artwork. Sometimes one has the opportunity to choose a site specifically for its significance to a particular project, as I was able to do for my self-initiated *GERNIKA/GUERNICA* project. At

other times, there is less flexibility in siting the project. In these situations, finding
and bringing to light the site's contributions to the work is more challenging, and
not every artist will be up to the task. This is often a matter of compatibility, not
lack of experience or ability. Sometimes a site simply responds more to particular
style or medium. For example, the High Line Park functions better as a space for
sound-based rather than physical interventions, as evidenced by Steven Vitiello's
successful temporary sound installation there, *A Bell for Every Minute*. In these
situations, an artist relies on arts administrators to help judge whether he or she is
a good match for a particular site. It is thus not only artists who must pay attention
to the site and respond carefully to its specific needs and contributions; responding
to a public site must be a collaborative process undertaken both by the artist and
by the administrative team responsible for the project.

In this increasingly object-oriented and mercantile art world, artists are beginning to think and work at other ways in which they can contribute their talents to
society. Artists are creating public works in locations that were previously inacces-
sible and interacting with audience populations that have never before experienced
public art in this way. Fresh and unusual mediums are being integrated into public
spaces, effectively transforming them into thought-provoking and interactive experiences of "place." Yet site responsiveness is not the sole purview of the artist.
It is only with the support of arts administrators that public art has been able to
move in this experimental direction. And, of course, public art would be nowhere
without an audience of people to respond to it—with criticism, praise, or indifference. Whether public art becomes someone's home or a table for lunch or inspires
an utterly different perspective on the world, it will keep moving forward. Let's see
what we can accomplish together.

2

Public Art in the Hands of the Public Realm

K. M. Williamson

INTRODUCTION

Humorous meddling, contentious protests, indiscriminate vandalism, and even indifference can all present difficult challenges for communities wishing to protect public art investments and reaffirm their community art programs and civic life. How public art looks, where it has been placed, how it makes people feel or not feel, how it attracts unintended or undesirable activity or attracts no activity at all—these are the concerns of both the local community and the wider public realm. Although public art programs may anticipate some degree of postinstallation repair or maintenance, understanding different forms and degrees of civic engagement with public art in situ can help cities and communities counteract potential distress and damage to public art, to the public space, to the community, and even to the surrounding public realm.

Public art programs have long proven their value as effective templates for enriching communities with cultural amenities, and we celebrate their ability to serve so many more community-enhancing functions than the mere provision of artworks. The public art process, however, can be so extensive that communities and stakeholders hail the artwork's installation as the program's finale rather than the beginning of a new and dynamic stage of public reaction and response. This postinstallation stage is where artwork truly becomes *public art*, as it is exposed for the first time to the thoughts and feelings of a diverse public realm. This resulting civic engagement of public responses can therefore tell us much about successful or problematic areas of a community's public art program and effort.

This chapter reviews a variety of public responses to public art installations from the past decade that illustrate forms and degrees of civic engagement with public art. By classifying public responses along a civic engagement continuum

13

ranging in intensity from public enthusiasm and criticism to public indifference and ignorance, we explore the roots of such engagement residing within public art programs and processes. Examining the nature of this civic engagement with public art illustrates program strengths and weaknesses that can then be addressed with program corrections and policy revisions.

CIVIC ENGAGEMENT WITH PUBLIC ART

Most public art programs across America now make concerted efforts to involve communities in public art selection, creation, and location decisions. The general view, however, that civic and community engagement is most relevant at these *pre-installation* stages is shortsighted. It is the *post-installation* public art and public space dynamic that provides a community with its most diverse, intense, and authentic civic engagement context and communication opportunity.

One of public art's most compelling functions is its role as a civic message "beacon" that serves the communicative context of the public realm (Knight 2008, 23): public art expresses who and what the community is and wants to be. It is the public realm of ever-shifting density and diversity that responds to, modifies, and ultimately ratifies or rejects the proffered public art and its meaning (Senie 2003, 188–90, 197). Howsoever a community plans for a public artwork's form and message, once it is installed in public, its subsequent meaning and relevance are inherently dependent on the surrounding physical and social context. Public responses therefore have the power to either enhance or threaten the success of the public art, the public space, and even the community itself.

How can this post-installation civic engagement be anticipated and supported so that community efforts and investments are safeguarded and enhanced? Four types of public responses are analyzed for how various public art efforts may or may not have been mindful of their effects.

AN ENGAGEMENT CONTINUUM: FROM ENTHUSIASM AND CRITICISM TO INDIFFERENCE AND IGNORANCE

The most highly publicized responses to public art are naturally those that are most intense. When public responses are positive and supportive, they celebrate, confirm, and enhance the public art and surrounding public realm. When negative and critical, they can foment contention and disappointment as they call for changes to the artwork's form, message, or to the chosen location. Intense public responses, even when critical, are nevertheless highly engaged with the public art *as public art*.

At the other end of the engagement continuum are public responses so mild that they reflect near indifference to the public art—where installation ceremonies are unattended and both public art and space are soon forgotten and abandoned. Beyond indifference, we find public responses so fundamentally unengaged as to seem entirely ignorant of the public art *as public art*. Indiscriminate vandalism and theft imply that the public art is treated as merely structure and material. Such indifference and ignorance toward a community's public art effort may not immediately attract the news media, but the likely consequences of neglect and deterioration are nearly always exposed and publicized.

The public realm's civic engagement with public art can therefore be positively or negatively intense (with enthusiastic responses or critical responses) as well as positively or negatively mild (with indifferent responses or ignorant responses).

High Civic Engagement: Enthusiastic and Critical Public Responses

Enthusiastic public reactions are indisputable testimonies of program success: the sculpture or mural is deemed charming and attractive, the message is perceived as interesting or laudable, the space is felt to be enhanced, and the community and general public appear to enjoy and embrace it. Such successful program outcomes deserve celebration but also continued monitoring, because the dynamic, diverse, and often unpredictable public realm can easily shift its perceptions and attitudes. Initial reactions toward a particular public artwork can change in both intensity and direction over time, especially as diverse interests gravitate toward public art to vie for exposure and influence. Even if Honolulu's *Duke Kahanamoku* statue at Waikiki Beach was installed in a way to best attract photo-taking tourists instead of to reflect Hawaiian custom, its subsequent success with local residents and tourists alike as a cultural icon has cemented its sacred status. It now serves as a paramount symbol of Hawaii's island hospitality and a focus of community events (Chan and Feeser 2006).

In a similar sense, the City of New York could hardly have anticipated Robert Indiana's *LOVE* sculpture on Sixth Avenue becoming one of the country's most popular photo-op destinations for couples and newlyweds (FoundAroundNYC 2006). Civic engagement with public art can therefore become theme based and even event driven, such as with South Pasadena's large *Astride-Aside* walking man sculpture adorned with paper-chain necklaces in celebration of Earth Day 2014 (see figure 2.1).

When public art is redefined by the public realm, the additional or different messages attached to it can also reflect special or private interests. Enthusiastic civic engagement can become more narrow, aggressive or politically driven. The risk of public art being coopted by an uncivic message is ever present, and communities are wise to carefully monitor both the legality and civic mindedness of diverse public responses. We find an interesting example of community-enhancing civic engagement in Encinitas, California, where a sculpture at a highly visible traffic intersection initially attracted strong criticism but over time became a focus for humorous and spontaneous jokes and messages.

Figure 2.1.　Astride-Aside

Matthew Antichevich's *Magic Carpet Ride* sculpture of a novice surfer attracted strong criticism as soon as it was installed in 2007. Local surfers argued that it was both confusing (in a technical surfing sense) and unflattering to the local Encinitas surfing community. Soon the large bronze sculpture with conveniently outstretched arms was dubbed *The Cardiff Kook* and subjected to an ongoing series of costumes, signs, and embellishments that compete for novelty and amusement. Considering its initially negative reception, it now functions as a community beacon (see figure 2.3) and attracts local events such as the Cardiff Kook 10k Run, much to the surprise of both the artist and city officials (Dougherty 2010). The public response of pranks has not damaged the sculpture, although the sculpture and site may be at risk of becoming a publicity-stunt locale for other private or special interests that may prove difficult to control.

Cities and communities should therefore keep in mind the possibility that their public art may attract interests that are not community minded and that such public responses have consequences for community well-being as well as the public art in

Figure 2.2. Florence Nightingale—damaged

question. Careful judgment and/or swift action may be necessary to keep "place-making" efforts from being sacrificed to "place-taking" interests.

When communities encounter negative responses to public art, they should consider them as also reflecting a high degree of civic engagement with the public artwork, its form and meaning, and the surrounding context. Public criticism, so often influenced by current events, still emerges from a public art context of communication with the community. With the expectation that criticism will be heard and responded to, public responses are often specific and remedy suggesting. Criticism of public art therefore does not imply a complete or fundamental failure of the public art program and process. If administrators and program staff carefully consider the substance of negative responses, they are likely to learn thoughtful and effective suggestions that could quickly salvage and even improve the public art effort. The following examples illustrate how targeted and remedy-suggesting negative public responses can be formulated.

Negative responses often target the appropriateness of an artwork's site because of a particular undesirable meaning produced by the artwork-site context. They often suggest removing the public art to another locale where the undesirable meaning would not exist. The notable case of Michael Brohman's *Journey* sculpture in Colorado Springs, Colorado, made this distinction clear. When *Journey* was installed in front of the El Paso County Courthouse, its depiction of an African slave ship, with faceless black figures forming the spines of the ship, was strongly evocative. While the theme and quality of the artwork were widely celebrated, its placement at the courthouse created a modern-day association between black slavery and the disproportionate number of incarcerated blacks in the criminal justice system. Public responses unanimously called for relocating the artwork to avoid this context-based meaning (Mobley-Martinez 2010).

In a smaller setting, students at Wellesley College similarly criticized the location of public art installed near a highly visible pathway. The *Sleepwalker* sculpture of a lifelike middle-aged man wearing only underwear and stumbling as if in a trance was part of an exhibit at the nearby Davis Museum, yet the artist chose to place it instead in the snow near a dormitory pathway. Students quickly found the contextual meaning of menace and threat near their residence too unexpected and unnerving and petitioned to have it removed and reinstalled at the museum building's context of "art display" (Reiss 2014).

Like the surfing community's initial reaction to *The Cardiff Kook*, negative public responses show a keen sensitivity to public art's impact on community reputation. In Saskatoon, Saskatchewan, residents were upset to discover that the recently installed public art for their neighborhood, touted as a site-specific work sponsored by the city's Placemaker Art Program, was an artist's statement on waste management (Pender 2013). *Found Compressions One and Two*, a large two-piece work of compressed and bundled trash, was installed on a residential street corner and immediately encountered community objections regarding the statement it made about their neighborhood. One outraged homeowner covered the piece with a tarpaulin and attached his own note of complaint that the artwork looked like "abandoned garbage" and tarnished the neighborhood's image. Although the artist's intended message of promoting recycling was widely acknowledged, in the residential context the message indeed felt "place specific"—and insulting. Residents insisted it be removed and installed at a municipal locale (CBC News 2014). These public responses clearly distinguished the artwork's originally intended meaning from the meaning produced by the residential siting choice.

Some public art messages, however, are so strong and inherent to the artwork itself that criticisms can't easily be satisfied by relocating the artwork elsewhere. In such cases, negative responses usually suggest problems in earlier public art program stages, and a recurring theme is the degree and nature of community oversight. A recent example of inadequate public oversight is found in the Michigan city of Adrian's installation and subsequent removal of its *Blue Human Condition* sculpture. The piece attracted media notoriety after widespread community objections that it contained too much "sexual innuendo." A description of the sculpture answers why: blue-tinted naked humanoid figures are shown resting on top of, pressing on, and folding over each other in tight configuration with what could be perceived as sexually suggestive proximity. Even though *Blue Human Condition* was planned as a temporary installation at the Adrian City Hall, the community nevertheless had no involvement in the selection and siting, nor did they have advance notice of the temporary public art program and its duration. An independent arts organization outside the city, Midwest Sculpture Initiative, had contracted with city officials for a temporary public art exhibit of several artworks (City of Adrian 2014). Unfortunately, no city or community representative knew about or approved the *Blue Human Condition* choice (Panian 2014; Gable 2014). Although city officials expressed dismay that their community or the general public could reasonably perceive a sexual message in it instead of the intended message of "mutual support," it is reasonable to assume that civic or community involvement in selection and siting decisions would have anticipated the subsequent objections.

Another example of limited community oversight illustrates how political messages can make their way into public art in seemingly innocent ways. Public art messages can include a political subtext, often stemming from an artist's or sponsor's personal agenda and likely to attract public criticism and contention. Such was the case with a "cultural diversity" mural in Wichita, Kansas, that was vandalized twice in a three-month period with racist and anti-Semitic graffiti (Eckels 2013). It is unclear whether the community mural effort by a local artist aiming to "elevate a lively spirit of justice and colorful cultural expression" was ever conceptually approved by any civic entity. The completed mural, however, depicted the struggles of Mexican immigrants in entering the United States, fronted by the title *Immigration Is Beautiful* in bold letters. The lead artist subsequently described the mural as having been designed to convey a pro-immigration message currently being debated in the media (Finger 2014). If the Wichita mural creation process had incorporated community-based public review, the mural's final images and message may well have been guided away from a controversial political position.

We can see that the negative public responses to the compressed trash *Found Compressions One and Two* and the *Blue Human Condition* sculpture did not imply an utter public art program failure. However much earlier decisions may have erred, the civic engagement effort proposed effective solutions. Prompt siting changes can rectify undesirable context-based public art meaning or messages. Where there are strong objections to an artwork's inherent meaning or message, effective solutions short of the artwork's complete removal may be more difficult to find (such as with Wichita's *Immigration Is Beautiful* mural). Nevertheless, public art programs can learn from and adjust to what were formerly unknown community reactions and concerns as well as to specific community oversight missteps in the public art process.

Low Civic Engagement: Indifferent and Ignorant Public Responses

With high civic engagement, enthusiastic and critical public responses are fairly tangible—approval, enjoyment, objections, or distress are expressed through word or action and easily telegraphed by the media. With low degrees of civic engagement, indifferent and ignorant public responses can follow a more subtle and more destructive path. Although general indifference to public art translates to few tangible public responses, such indifference still tacitly accepts and acknowledges the validity of the public art process and outcome. The worse danger lies in how indifference to public art can easily fade over time to a degree of ignorance that no longer recognizes or appreciates it *as public art*. When we see public responses like theft or indiscriminate vandalism, we are impressed by the fundamental lack of awareness of the artwork's "public" and "artistic" status and value. The lowest level of civic engagement with public art is therefore illustrated by public responses that appraise it and approach it as merely physical structure or material.

Contrary to the popular adage, no news about a community's public art is definitely not good news. Indifferent public responses to newly installed or long-standing public art can signal that the community and the public may at the very least be confused as to whether any degree of civic engagement is warranted. At the heart of such low civic engagement may be the question of whether the public art seems to actually belong to the community.

First and foremost, communities ask themselves whether an artwork is indeed *their* public art—reflecting *their* community and worthy of their stewardship (Francis 1989). Where there is general indifference, public art may be tacitly accepted as public art but not embraced as especially meaningful or relevant.

Indifference can emerge over time when the public art meaning or message becomes too irrelevant to a new and different culture, despite any earlier enthusiasm that may have surrounded the artwork's creation. Historic statues and sculptures representing another era's values can be especially vulnerable to indifferent or ignorant public responses, like neglect and vandalism. Public responses to the Florence Nightingale statue in Los Angeles, California, illustrate this trajectory. Erected in

Figure 2.3. Magic Carpet Ride

1937 by the Federal Art Project and sponsored by the Hospital Council of Southern California, the seven-foot cast stone artwork complemented the nearby hospital and reflected the city's early public health efforts (see figure 2.2). The statue faded in civic importance by the 1960s and 1970s after civil rights and Mexican cultural issues dominated the East Los Angeles neighborhood. Despite ongoing and notable damage and vandalism (graffiti, poor repair), the statue attracted almost no public responses over the decades. A couple of private nursing schools once expressed interest in the statue, but only to obtain it for free and remove it to private property and ownership (Lopez 2014).

Public art located in distant locations or in restricted, semiprivate locations is also vulnerable to indifferent public responses. When public art is located inside government offices or corporate lobbies, it can be too detached from the community and public realm to encourage civic engagement. Many mid-twentieth-century public artworks, for example, were sponsored by private businesses and placed in building lobbies. Many have been nearly lost to public indifference, such as the locally inspired Millard Sheets mosaics on Southern California Home Savings and Loan building interiors and exteriors (Los Angeles Conservancy Modern Committee 2012). In many cases, public artworks in such private and interior locations were often forgotten until after they had been removed and destroyed by subsequent building owners and tenants (Pasadena Independent 2009). Indifferent responses can therefore stem from a location-based confusion about whether an artwork is truly public art and whether it indeed belongs to a community.

Ignorant public responses take the form of indiscriminate vandalism or theft that approaches public art as merely commodity or item—material that has market value or structure that lends itself to marring or destruction. The low degree of civic engagement with public art shown by thefts and vandalism, however, can be revived with community outreach that educates and promotes interest. After Coeur d'Alene, Idaho, published community-wide pleas and informational editorials for the return of a stolen bronze heron sculpture, it reappeared within a week (Hasslinger 2011). And in Los Angeles, the theft of a historic Henry Lion bronze sculpture, *Miner*, from a traffic median caused the neighborhood to reflect on what had been a long-neglected sculpture. Installed in 1925, its companion fountain designed as a mountain stream had long been inoperative and later removed. When the sculpture disappeared, however, the surrounding neighborhood was galvanized into action by fears that it would be destroyed for its scrap value. A community search located the piece before it was completely destroyed, and community officials turned its reinstallation into a civic engagement-building rededication ceremony that symbolized the successful thwarting of public art theft (Mozingo and Blankstein 2008).

Efforts to revive indifferent civic engagement when public art is damaged or stolen tend to have less success as time progresses and the event is forgotten. A bronze statue of Taras Shevshenko stolen from an Oakville, Ontario, park in 2001 suggests that a police investigation and a "no questions asked" $10,000 reward were not effective enough in locating either the thieves or the statue. Its reappearance ten years later on the fine art market prompted an art dealer, ignorant of the theft, to contact the Taras Shevchenko Museum rather than the Oakville city officials or police (Kennedy 2012). In Enumclaw, Washington, ongoing vandalism of a sculpture that had both structural and authorship concerns from the outset finally led to its demise and removal. Civic engagement with the public art was compromised early on when the sculpture arrived already damaged and a debate ensued about its authenticity (Vane 2007). *Boys in the Band* was made of lightweight bronze and iron, and the city found that appendages were easily broken off. The indiscriminate vandalism left the broken-off pieces where they fell, implying the artwork's worthlessness as public art to the vandals (Duchateau 2014).

Whether the more destructive public responses of theft and vandalism are motivated by private gain or senseless destruction, they nevertheless illustrate that the public art effort has, at least initially, failed to reach and impress a segment of the community or broader public. These public responses also suggest that the intensity, immediacy, and educational quality of a community's response to public art theft and vandalism can be effective in counteracting indifference and reviving civic engagement.

PLANNING FOR POST-INSTALLATION CIVIC ENGAGEMENT

Maintaining Process Integrity with Local Oversight

Communities are engaged by public art that resonates with their idea and understanding of the civic world around them. The *Found Compressions One and Two* bundled trash sculpture, *The Cardiff Kook* novice surfer sculpture, and the *Blue Human Condition* naked blue humans sculpture all attracted critical public responses objecting to unappealing images and messages being attributed to them and their community. These public responses illustrated how adept communities and the public can be at sensing context-based meaning. Perhaps predictably, each community's public art process omitted local oversight, especially by the community segment that was to host the public art.

Public art that is proposed, created, and sponsored by either individual artists or private organizations without local public oversight risks the economic investment and community trust while inviting contention or apathy. Too often we hear criticism that public art is the right art but in the wrong place, leaving cities with the costly task of removing the artwork to another locale. Involving the hosting community at the earliest program stages clearly has future benefits in identifying issues that can promote the artwork and space as successful community assets. The hosting community should therefore be identified as key stakeholders and play a significant role in the public art creation and siting process.

Planning for the Post-Installation Stage of Public Response

A useful caution about the public realm is that change is inherent and unavoidable (Lofland 1998, 71). This does not mean that such change must occur quickly or that change will be for the worse. Vigilant monitoring of community and public responses to public art can help identify emerging changes in behavior and attitudes early enough for review and corrections. This means that public art programs can enhance and guide the broad enjoyment of public art with community events and programming. It also means that special, political, or otherwise undesirable "coopting" of public art can be curtailed or redirected before it can become deeply entrenched. Critical responses, instead of being avoided or discounted, can be seriously considered and incorporated as potentially effective solutions. And when communities encounter the lowest civic engagement of indifference and ignorance, subsequent public outreach and education can renew the meaning and value of both public art and public space for the "hosting" community as well as for the general public.

Planning Comprehensively: Public Art, Public Space, and Public Realm

Since public art meaning is so dependent on the physical and social space that hosts it, the importance of planning art, space, and social life in tandem cannot be overstated. Post-installation management plans should be comprehensive in coordinating public art and public space maintenance and programming, with a flexibility to respond to the dynamic social needs of the public realm (Fleming 2007, 295). Kendellen and Krueger present a preliminary template for registering public art maintenance issues that at least acknowledges the potential of human interaction with public art (2005, 225). A more comprehensive approach, however, is essential in order to support the combined benefits of art and space. Physical elements such as artwork material, lighting, and special effects should be coordinated with space landscaping and furniture maintenance so that mutually enhancing features, such as fountains or kinetic components, continue to be effective. Perceptible deterioration in either artwork or space signals a disinvestment in both and risks the "broken windows" effect of neglect and civic disengagement (Wilson and Kelling 1982).

Management of the social features of both artwork and space should also be coordinated with an eye toward supporting a civic-engaged public realm. Public art naturally attracts and is often designed for physical interaction, and the surrounding public space provides the highly desirable "see and be seen" context that community programming can build on. Programming both public art and the public realm can enhance a sense of place and build cultural traditions, to say nothing of promoting support for the arts in general. Festivals, farmers markets, and chamber of commerce programs and events can highlight and celebrate both public art and public space.

Promotional efforts can expand beyond traditional publicity releases and instead reorient toward community education and cultural programs while also targeting audiences beyond the local arts community. Informational materials, public art receptions, and tours are basic components of a community's public art education program (Piechocki 2005). The City of Honolulu's efforts reflect such comprehensive public art planning: cultural and community events are focused around the nine-foot *Duke Kahanamoku* statue, including lei draping ceremonies, all captured by a twenty-four-hour live web camera (City and County of Honolulu 2014). Honolulu then built on their public art and cultural program efforts by installing *The Stones of Life* monument nearby, a grouping of three sacred ancient healing stones or boulders (sometimes referred to as "wizard stones") as an additional focus of Hawaiian spirituality and culture (Chan and Feeser 2006, 78).

Coordinating these interconnected public art/public space management plans requires effective cooperation between municipal departments (facilities, planning, cultural resources) that can access and update a comprehensive data management tool. A cultural assets inventory coordinated between a variety of municipal departments can serve as a valuable data tracking tool in recording valuable installation details, artwork and site maintenance, improvements, and programming efforts. To this list should be added the tracking of formal and informal public responses to both artwork and space so that the most effective adjustments can be made (Fleming 2007, 320). Such an inventory can promote efficiency as well as effective policy. It might also have saved the City of Vallejo, California, from losing track of several public sculptures installed in the 1960s when disrupted by a large redevelopment project. The artworks were placed in storage for safekeeping and ultimately forgotten and lost. Even though the city received numerous inquiries over the years, reflecting a notable degree of civic engagement with the public art, many pieces were lost due to poor records and high staff turnover (Burchyns 2014). Registering and consistently reviewing public art and public spaces as bona fide municipal and community assets can provide cities with an essential tool in avoiding their loss and neglect.

IN THE HANDS OF THE PUBLIC REALM

Enthusiastic responses to public art are naturally the most expected and desirable program outcomes, but communities would be wise to not rest on their laurels of success without planning for subsequent and inevitable shifts in the public realm's civic engagement intensity and direction. And although no program administrator looks forward to critical responses, careful and prompt attention to such feedback can help identify effective solutions and avoid contention and negative publicity. Where there is any degree of public response, there is civic engagement; and where there is civic engagement, there exists the public realm's advantages of dialogue and mutual understanding.

Indifference and ignorance toward public art should never imply that any public understanding and appreciation of the public art and program effort exists. This examination of the variety and nature of public responses tells us that an absence of civic engagement with public art is fateful for both artwork and community: it impeaches the public art process of community oversight and undermines public art stewardship, thereby risking investments in both art and space. This alone should sufficiently argue the value of planning for civic engagement with public art, but the more compelling advantages of place making and civil society are within reach of a public art planning policy more sensitive to the dynamics of the public realm.

LIST OF REFERENCED PUBLIC ART

Astride-Aside. 2003. Michael Stutz. Location: park adjacent to Metro Gold Line South Pasadena Station, 905 Meridian Avenue, South Pasadena, CA.

Blue Human Condition. 2014. Mark Chatterly. Location: Yew Park, Winter Street (north of Maumee Street), Adrian, MI.

Boys in the Band. 2014. Jim Davidson [disputed]. Location, 2007–2014: Enumclaw City Hall, Porter Street and Griffin Avenue, Enumclaw, WA. Removed and destroyed 2014.

Duke Kahanamoku. 1990. Jan Gordon Fisher. Location: Kuhio Beach Park at Uluniu Avenue, Honolulu, HI.

Found Compressions One and Two. 2014. Keeley Haftner. Location, April 2014: 33rd Street and Avenue "C." Saskatoon, Ontario, Canada.

Immigration Is Beautiful. 2014. Armando Minjarez and students. Location: 21st Street and Park Place, Wichita, KS.

Journey. 2002. Michael Brohman. Location, 2010: El Paso County Courthouse, Colorado Springs, CO. Location 2012: Auraria Campus, Denver, CO.

LOVE. Date unknown. Robert Indiana. Location: 1359 Avenue of the Americas (at Sixth Avenue), New York, NY.

Miner. 1925. Henry Lion. Location: Carthay Circle, corner of San Vicente Blvd. and McCarthy Vista, Los Angeles, CA.

Magic Carpet Ride (The Cardiff Kook). 2007. Matthew Antichevich. Location: entrance to San Elijo State Beach campground, South Coast Highway, *Cardiff-by-the-Sea*, Encinitas, CA.

Sleepwalker. 2014. Tony Matelli. Part of *New Gravity* exhibition. Location: Davis Museum, Wellesley College, Massachusetts.

The Stones of Life (Nā Pōhaku Ola O Kapaemahu A Me Kapuni). Circa 1500; installed 1997. Location: Kuhio Beach Park at Uluniu Avenue, Honolulu, HI.

Taras Shevshenko. 1951. Ivan Honchar. Current location: Taras Schevshenko Museum, 1614 Bloor Street West, Toronto, Ontario, Canada.

REFERENCES

Burchyns, Tony. 2014. "Vallejo Citizens Urge City to Restore Forgotten Public Art." *Times-Herald.* October 17. Accessed October 21, 2014. http://www.timesheraldonline.com/portal/breaking_news/ci_26752012/vallejo-citizens-urge-city-restore-forgotten-public-art?_loop back=1.

CBC News. 2014. "Saskatoon Resident Tarps over 'Unsightly' Public Art." *CBC News.* April 22. Accessed April 24, 2014. http://www.cbc.ca/news/canada/saskatoon/saskatoon -resident-tarps-over-unsightly-public-art-1.2617828.

Chan, Gaye, and Andrea Feeser. 2006. *Waikiki: A History of Forgetting and Remembering.* Honolulu: University of Hawaii Press.

City of Adrian. 2014. "Adrian Art Discovery." *City of Adrian, Michigan.* Accessed October 14, 2014. http://adriancity.com/community/adrian-art-discovery/.

City and County of Honolulu. 2014. "Waikiki Beach Live Camera." Accessed October 23, 2014. http://www1.honolulu.gov/multimed/waikiki.asp.

Dougherty, Conor. 2010. "Surfer Statue Stokes Gnarly Controversy in California. The 'Kook' Gets Dressed as a Clown, Eaten by a Shark." *Wall Street Journal.* August 31. Accessed October 23, 2014. http://online.wsj.com/articles/SB10001424052748703369704575462022661106574.

Duchateau, Wally. 2014. "Vandals Too Much for Public Art." *Enumclaw Courier-Herald.* April 17. Accessed May 20, 2014. http://www.courierherald.com/community/255692491.html.

Eckels, Carla. 2013. "New Mural In North Wichita Depicts Immigration Struggles." *Wichita Public Radio KMUW.* October 24. Accessed February 20, 2014. http://kmuw.org/post/ new-mural-north-wichita-depicts-immigration-struggles.

Finger, Stan. 2014. "Grassroots Art Group's Leader Reacts to Mural Vandalism." *Wichita Eagle.* February 13. Accessed February 20, 2014. http://newsinkansas.com/grassroots-art -groups-leader-reacts-to-mural-vandalism/.

Fleming, Ronald Lee. 2007. *The Art of Placemaking: Interpreting Community through Public Art and Urban Design.* New York: Merrill.

FoundAroundNYC. 2006. "LOVE Sculpture." Retrieved from http://foundaroundnyc.type pad.com/found_around_nyc/2006/09/love_sculpture.html.

Gable, Erik. 2014. "As 'Save the Blue Humans' Movement Grows, City Holds Off on Sculpture's Removal." *Adrian Today.* April 25. Accessed April 26, 2014. http://adriantoday .com/2014/04/25/as-save-the-blue-humans-movement-grows-city-holds-off-on-sculptures -removal/250.

Hasslinger, Tom. 2011. "Stolen Heron Art Returned." *CDA Press.* November 6. Accessed January 15, 2012. http://www.cdapress.com/news/local_news/article_3de39ac3–95e0 –5a73–be48–f7660e0b36d4.html.

Kendellen, Peggy, and Robert Krueger. 2005. "The Nuts and Bolts of a Maintenance Program." In *Public Art by the Book,* edited by Barbara Goldstein, 212–34. Seattle: University of Washington Press.

Kennedy, Brendan. 2012. "Stolen Taras Shevchenko Statue Returned after 10 Years." *Toronto Star.* February 5. Accessed May 20, 2012. http://www.thestar.com/news/gta/2012/02/05/ stolen_taras_shevchenko_statue_returned_after_10_years.html.

Knight, Cher Krause. 2008. *Public Art: Theory, Practice and Populism.* Malden: Blackwell.

Lofland, Lyn H. 1998. *The Public Realm: Exploring the City's Quintessential Social Territory.* Hawthorne, NY: Aldine de Gruyter.

Lopez, Steve. 2014. "Battered Florence Nightingale Statue Needs Critical Care." *Los Angeles Times.* February 8. Accessed February 8, 2014. http://articles.latimes.com/2014/feb/08/ local/la-me-0209-lopez-florence-20140208.

Los Angeles Conservancy Modern Committee. 2012. "Millard Sheets: A Legacy of Art and Architecture." *Los Angeles Conservancy.* Accessed October 24, 2014. http://lac.laconser vancy.org/site/DocServer/millard_sheets_booklet.pdf?docID=981.

Mobley-Martinez, T. D. 2010. "Downtown Sculpture Depicting African Slave Ship Starts Controversy." *Gazette.* March 6. Accessed April 24, 2014. http://gazette.com/downtown-sculp ture-depicting-african-slave-ship-starts-controversy/article/95238#xGtsqdiATM6Qppf5.99.

Mozingo, Joe, and Andrew Blankstein. 2008. "Police Strike Pay Dirt in Hunt for Stolen Statue of Miner." *Los Angeles Times.* February 16. Accessed March 18, 2010. http://articles.latimes .com/2008/feb/16/local/me-statue16.

Panian, David. 2014. "Sculpture to Be Replaced after Complaints of Sexual Innuendo." *Daily Telegram.* April 24. Accessed April 25, 2014. http://www.lenconnect.com/article/ 20140424/News/140429487.

Pasadena Independent. 2009. "Relocation of Bank's Millard Sheets Mural Under Discussion." *Pasadena Independent.* December 21. Accessed December 23, 2009. http://www.pasadena independent.com/news/relocation-of-banks-millard-sheets-mural-under-discussion/.

Pender, Greg. 2013. "City Employees Install 'Found Compressions One and Two' . . ." *Star Phoenix, Montreal Gazette.* November 28. Accessed October 27, 2014. http:// www.montrealgazette.com/City+employees+install+Found+Compressions+Keeley+Haft ner+site+specific+sculpture+consisting+cellophane+wrapped+bales+valueless+compacted +plastics+corner+Avenue+33rd+Street+West+Friday+work+part+city+Placemaker+prog ram/9228123/story.html.

Piechocki, Renee. 2005. "Beyond the Ribbon Cutting: Education and Programming Strategies for Public Art Projects and Programs." In *Public Art by the Book,* edited by Barbara Goldstein, 192–209. Seattle: University of Washington Press.

Reiss, Jaclyn. 2014. "Statue of Sleep-Walking Man Triggers Controversy at Wellesley College." *Boston Globe.* February 6. Accessed February 10, 2014. http://www.bostonglobe.com/ metro/2014/02/06/statue-sleepwalking-man-triggers-controversy-wellesley-college/cTvPc-GKDnExMs1bp0mnrzJ/story.html.

Senie, Harriet. 2003. "Reframing Public Art: Audience Use, Interpretation, and Appreciation." In *Art and Its Publics: Museum Studies at the Millennium*, edited by Andrew McClellan, 185–200. Malden: Blackwell.

Vane, Lauren. 2007. "Enumclaw Satisfied Suspect Sculpture Is the Real Deal." *Seattle Times, Times Southeast Bureau*. August 24. Accessed October 30, 2014. http://seattletimes.com/html/localnews/2003850993_sculpture24m.html.

Wilson, James Q., and George L. Kelling. 1982. "Broken Windows: The Police and Neighborhood Safety." *Atlantic Monthly*, March, 29–38.

II

BUILDING PUBLIC ART
THAT UNITES AND
DEFINES COMMUNITIES

3

Building Civic Engagement through Urban Public Art

Donna Isaac

INTRODUCTION

Art has played a significant role in forming the character, traditions, and heritage of Scottsdale. The city became known regionally as the center for arts and culture in the greater Valley of the Sun that encompasses the larger Phoenix metropolitan area. The city's public art organization, Scottsdale Public Art, has made enormous strides in its almost thirty years. The aesthetic character and quality of the downtown urban infrastructure, the invitation to residents and tourists to experience Scottsdale, and the investment by the city in the downtown Scottsdale waterfront helped the city to mark itself as unique while drawing millions of visitors annually to stay, recreate, and visit.

Community is integral to public art. Art in the public realm invites public critique, pleasure, surprise, discussion, and controversy. As an urban public art program, Scottsdale Public Art has encountered all of these. Public art can often strengthen community attachment and involvement with the arts and equally as often widen the divide between art perceived as elitist and its public, who question taxpayer dollars spent on art. Public art reflects the changing tastes and attitudes of a city, its government and citizenry, as well as the civic attitudes of the populous. We can all too often dissemble how a city develops dialogue with its citizens. It is easy to believe that as public art administrators we encourage feedback from the interested public through surveys and community interface at public meetings. The reality is that community engagement, awareness, and advocacy for public art is built not only through its perceived successes but also through controversy, dialogue, and difficult conversations that often focus on those works of art less generally understood or tolerated. Civic engagement is built on trust, which develops over time and through the strength of civic relationships.

31

Public art, like all creative disciplines, reflects the period in which it was created. A program that has a broad spectrum reflects this depth. It is equally imperative that public art respond to changes in the community and embrace them. Changing demographics, changing values, changing policies and economics, and changes in technology all influence approaches to art. Ultimately for those programs, like Scottsdale Public Art, with a percent for art ordinance, civic dialogue and engagement also takes place at the polls—voting for the capital improvement bonds program that in turn support public art projects.

LEVELS OF COMMUNITY ENGAGEMENT

Community is an amorphous term but one that has great importance to a discipline that is so wide, so divergent in tastes, and so political. While it may take a village to build a public artwork, it also takes the village to finally embrace it and make it their own. A public art program must engage the community to both build the program and help them to make it their own. There are different levels of engaging community and as many ways to assess the community experience. Art begs an individual response. Yet public art as a discipline looks at a much larger and longer view, and here lies the heart of the matter regarding community engagement.

Quantifying community engagement is challenging for a public art program. How does one know how to quantify art in the public, which touches all those who encounter it each day? Any estimate goes beyond mere numbers and in most cases cannot even be exact. Public art can cause change, very often without even the realization of this occurrence. Surveys and community meetings help to provide some quantifiable data. There is no easily understood way to assess the numbers. Public art is very often embedded and integral within urban design and becomes indistinguishable from the urban fabric of a city. Thus any dialogue with a government on the value of public art for a community can quickly lead to grey areas of established generalizations.

Engaging community with public art is, by way of definition, what public art does. Finding ways to assess this engagement has been at the forefront of Scottsdale Public Art's work. Over the past seven years, Scottsdale Public Art has established itself as a leader in community engagement—effectively embracing the public and engaging in dialogue and specific interactions, making it truly integral with public art and always looking at ways to measure the level of success of this engagement.

HISTORY

Scottsdale Public Art is located in Scottsdale, Arizona. The city currently has a population of 250,000 and an annual visitor rate of eight to nine million visitors a year. Scottsdale Public Art has had the advantage of location in a city recognized since the 1950s as a mecca for artists, designers, and other creative types. This foundation brought some legitimacy to eventually creating a public art program. Even in the decade before Scottsdale Public Art was formed, the City of Scottsdale had a municipal art collection. Scottsdale commissioned Louise Nevelson for her first work in the southwest United States with an early National Endowment for the Arts grant. Scottsdale matched the funding for her work, *Atmosphere and Environments XVIII*, as the artist titled it. The piece became part of the city's collection in 1973 and is a much-beloved work of public art known to the community as *Windows on the West*.

In 1985 Scottsdale was one of the earliest cities in Arizona to establish a public art program, with the adoption of a public art ordinance.[1] The ordinance focuses on the quality of the built environment and integration of public art into the urban infrastructure of the city. The public art ordinance is a defining statement for the city and continues to impact citizens and visitors on a daily basis.

Scottsdale has continued to grow its public art programming through continually addressing the needs of a growing city during the 1980s and early 1990s. Scottsdale passed a cultural improvement project ordinance in 1989 with a focus on art in private development. This ordinance mandates public art expenditures up to 1 percent by private developers in the downtown area. This private development ordinance was the first in the state of Arizona to remain in effect and one of the earliest in the country. In December 2012 Scottsdale's city council revised the private development ordinance to include multifamily housing as well as commercial development in the downtown and expanded the ordinance to the area of the Airpark in north Scottsdale. This latter area is one of the region's fastest-growing employment centers.

STRUCTURE

The organizational structure of the newly founded public art program was defined under the Scottsdale Cultural Council, a not-for-profit organization working under a multiyear contract with the city. The organization was designed by the city council to answer to a board of trustees made up of Scottsdale residents and influential corporate and civic leaders. This structure allowed the overarching arts and cultural organization for the city to be outside of city politics. The programmatic selections and approvals are accomplished through approval by the board of trustees rather than by Scottsdale City Council. The structure of a public art program, mandated by ordinance to administer the city's public art program under a 501(c)3 is a different model for a public art program. However, this structure has for nearly thirty years afforded great latitude in more dynamic and multifaceted programming and far greater citizen decision making through the Scottsdale Public Art Advisory Board structure.

Scottsdale Public Art has built a tradition of community engagement over its nearly three decades. This engagement is built on multiple levels of dialogue, beginning with an advisory board made up of residents, business owners, artists, architects, and landscape architects. The advisory board adds to the valuable discussions of individual projects and approves a yearly work plan established for each fiscal year. This advisory board also has the responsibility for approvals at critical junctures for each project. The advisory board plays a key role in supporting staff by participating in artist selection panels and approving budgets and artists' contracts.

Artist selection panels are critical to public outreach and are comprised of community members. This is done with city representatives along with citizens who are vocal about the proposed project, whether supporting or opposing it. This is important specifically for the particular context of the project. The artist selection panel includes architects, local artists, outside public art administrators, city representatives, and up to two representatives from the Scottsdale Public Art Advisory Board. The makeup of the selection panel is meant to provide a balanced viewpoint of the project, the context of the site, the community of users for the future project, and eventual ownership for the project.

All projects go out to the community at different stages and through various ways to receive input. After an artist selection, Scottsdale Public Art will engage the immediate community of users through a focus group. As the process continues with finalists' proposals and a final artist selection, Scottsdale Public Art once again gains valuable community input by encouraging people to view the proposals and answer questions related to the finalists' ideas for a project. This community engagement is prior to the final selection of the artist. Once selected, the artist is invited to engage with community through site visits, public meetings, and smaller-sized focus group meetings. The purpose of the engagement is to allow the artist to gain further information and valuable insight about the community or neighborhood. This is the opportunity for the artist to hear residents and business owners speak about their community and neighborhood and what is important.

Scottsdale Public Art participates in large public meetings with the city on specific projects. These meetings usually occur after the city design team has been selected. Scottsdale Public Art elicits community input with specific questions about the community and, along with the artist, engages the public in one-on-one discussions. This type of input is extended through social media to encourage community input using both the city and Scottsdale Public Art's websites and Facebook pages.

FLEXIBILITY IN PROGRAMMING

Scottsdale Public Art's programming through its nonprofit organization and the various funding streams ultimately creates much flexibility and provides its greatest opportunity in addressing the changing needs of the city and community. With the passage of Scottsdale's 2000 City Bond, the Art in Public Places (AIPP) fund was established. This separate stream of city funding has given the momentum for Scottsdale Public Art to expand its programming beyond the permanent, capital projects. Scottsdale Public Art has also begun to fund raise to support temporary and event-based installations while also building a strong record of grant making. The funding allows the program to engage the community and provide unexpected encounters with public art through temporary installations; a free, signature art event; and exhibitions that are curated.

The structure of a nonprofit has given this flexible dynamic, ultimately affording Scottsdale Public Art more opportunity to engage with local artists on interesting, cutting-edge projects and to engage the public with art on many different levels. The program helps to meet city needs by adding value to tourism. Drawing eight to nine million visitors a year makes Scottsdale unique in the valley and has helped to align the programming of its public art with other tourist-destination cities, such as Santa Monica, Santa Fe, San Diego, and San Francisco. Scottsdale recognizes the public art program is a tool for the city's economic and tourism competitiveness. Public art brings value to tourism development, education, and community development—all vital facets of civic life.[2] Scottsdale Public Art seeks to produce projects—especially temporary projects—in response to community needs. It was as a result of the economic downturn of 2008 and its tradition of responding to the changing needs of a city, as well as far less bond funding, that Scottsdale Public Art began to change its programming and refocused its direction on moving the program forward with temporary installations, a vibrant and growing exhibition program, and events.

Over nearly fifteen years, this foundation has provided a body of work that engages community through exhibitions, temporary installations in unexpected locations throughout the city, and events that activate the area of the Scottsdale waterfront. It is this flexible concept and unique approaches to programming that have resulted in not only greater community engagement and social practice but also the establishment of partnerships, which have included a public utility corporation. Below are examples of temporary installations that are the result of Scottsdale Public Art's ability to use its funding beyond permanent, capital-funded projects.

EXAMPLES OF TEMPORARY INSTALLATIONS

Red Ball

Early examples of temporary interactive projects began over six years ago. In 2008, Kurt Perschke's *Red Ball* project came to Scottsdale. This celebrated project gained global recognition and attention with prior appearances in Sydney, Australia; Barcelona, Spain; St. Louis, Missouri; and Portland, Oregon. In mid-January, *Red Ball* rolled into Scottsdale, Arizona, and for two weeks dotted the landscape, changing locations daily. Residents and visitors alike followed the project on Scottsdale Public Art's website and interacted through a photography competition. While the locations from bustling downtown urban Scottsdale sites to the serenity of the desert at Pinnacle Peak Park seemed random, the artist in fact chose them for his interactive work very carefully. "As public art that migrates, the *Red Ball* is a surrogate for the unique energy and character inherent at each unique site."[3]

Love Buttons

Gregory Sale's *Love Buttons* was a concept designed by the local Arizona artist and teacher as a participatory event for festivalgoers attending a rhythm-and-blues festival on a Sunday afternoon, April 6, 2008. Festival attendees were given buttons with printed text that included short phrases of encouragement. The buttons encouraged festival goers to interact with each other—possibly those wearing the same button or those whose buttons completed each other's phrases. People exchanged buttons with each other. Festival goers also engaged in the three "Have More Love" carts, where they could choose to exchange their buttons for others with one of forty-five different messages. The patterns of connection inherent in the poetic language were printed on signage attached to lampposts across the festival grounds. More than nine thousand buttons were distributed as a kind of wearable arts, which in turn became public art that was both interactive and performance art in nature. The project included local poets and spoken word artists. Part psychological experiment, part collaboration with strangers, and part a need to elicit intimacy, *Love Buttons* connected participants through chance encounters and linguistic association, all of which was intended to spark contemplation on love—its meaning and how we interact with it.[4]

Community Love

Volunteers helped to spread *Community Love*, a project by a local Arizona emerging artist, Jesse Fairchild, that drew the attention of motorists and pedestrians along Scottsdale Road on a single afternoon of March 24, 2010. During a previous afternoon, volunteers made dozens of signs with words the artist supplied and words they chose individually. The project, so simple by nature, was intriguing to those passersby who wanted information and who signaled their support. But it also engaged community with the participants both in the sign making and in the project—standing with a sign at corners along the twenty-four-mile Scottsdale Road. Some participants did more than hold signs—they interacted with the public. One couple who teaches tango took to the crosswalks to do just that. It reminded all of us that we are, in fact, part of a larger community, although we may pass each other every day with little of the kind of recognition that prevailed on that single afternoon in March.

The Marshall Project

One of the latest ideas to come about under the umbrella of Scottsdale Public Art's program of temporary installations, is the collaboration with the Scottsdale Museum of Contemporary Art to bring James Marshall, aka Dalek. The Marshall project is an example of how a collaboration such as this can result in a community mural. *Swish* is installed in an open, public space, the Belle Art Tower, at the offices of Scottsdale Public Art. Marshall demonstrates the strength of community building through his art. He works not only in close collaboration with community but also has the unique ability to listen to those who inhabit the space he is creating. The

Figure 3.1.   Artist Dalek with Community Nov. 2014

result, as pictured in the photograph in figure 3.1, is an energetic gathering in which the public creates alongside the artist for a truly meaningful public artwork. The second photograph (B) shows the community mural as it is installed in Scottsdale Pubic Art's temporary installation space, the Belle Art Tower.

Creative Residency

Developing a creative residency program for Scottsdale Public Art has been one of several initiatives considered to be pivotal to taking the program to another level of community engagement. A creative residency program has the capacity and ability to transcend static public art. Scottsdale Public Art has transformed an empty space in downtown Scottsdale into a lively, interactive arena. Preparing a proposal in response to a request for proposal issued by the City of Scottsdale for its city-owned Livery studio space, Scottsdale Public Art partnered with a downtown merchants association and the locally popular farmers market. This proved successful in convincing the city of the value of bringing together artists within the community. It developed an engaging and interactive series of programs that activated not only the actual space but an area of downtown Scottsdale that saw very little pedestrian traffic. In deciding to respond to the city's request for proposal, Scottsdale Public Art stepped outside the preconceived idea that as a quasi-city program, it did not need to show the value and merits of what a residency program could do for Scottsdale.

As a local artist program at this time, Scottsdale Public Art is building value in the idea of a residency program that crosses all the creative disciplines—writing, visual art, public art, photography, film, music, and so on. It is an exciting prospect still in its developing stages. The city council recently awarded two more years of free space for Scottsdale Public Art to continue to build and program this residency space. The council's decision is great acknowledgment indeed of the perceived value by the city in the work Scottsdale Public Art has undertaken.

INFLUX Initiative

With the economic downturn beginning in 2008, nearly a third of Scottsdale's galleries were closed, and boutiques and restaurants struggled. The INFLUX Initiative, launched in 2010, was an immediate response to the vacant spaces, empty areas, and brown-papered windowed storefronts that neither brought visitors nor encouraged pedestrian engagement along streets in downtown Scottsdale. The first cycle of this initiative, in 2010, focused on Scottsdale's Marshall Way Gallery District. Since the late 1980s, Marshall Way has provided contemporary galleries with well-known restaurants, individual and locally owned boutiques and gift shops, as well as public art. Marshall Way is a pedestrian-oriented street and has for nearly forty years hosted the Thursday night art walk. This Scottsdale Art Walk is one of the oldest in the nation. While at one time nearly twelve thousand people would walk along this street, the numbers have shrunk to barely a hundred. Much of this decrease has to do with the street no longer maintaining its presence as it tries to hold onto the concept of a gallery district.

The initiative provided Scottsdale Public Art with an opportunity to work with local artists to create intriguing and engaging installations in these empty spaces. While installations have been more passive in their artistic approaches, they still drew pedestrians and passersby along Marshall Way and gave them something to look at, to stop at along their route. Many installations have been purposefully interactive, intended to draw the public and the viewer even further into the world of the artist.

What INFLUX has achieved over the past four years is a remarkable mix of bringing attention to areas of the city with vacant spaces, empowering local artists to develop installations, establishing long-term partnerships with local property owners, and building a regional presence. INFLUX, in its current cycle, now incorporates eight regional cities and has done more through public art to reinvigorate areas and broaden community engagement with a long-term strategy to work with emerging artists than many other well-funded city and federal programs. More to the point, property owners contact Scottsdale Public Art to request the opportunity to participate. The public art installations through INFLUX are the foundation of significant public-private partnerships. INFLUX has enabled Scottsdale Public Art to move beyond the gallery district in downtown Scottsdale to areas of its edges with other cities, such as Tempe and Phoenix, and to expand to north Scottsdale.

The interactive nature of INFLUX has brought new community-building efforts. The events that surround INFLUX involve artists discussing their work on the street with the public, devising ways to engage public interest and feedback and even performance art in storefront windows. As the INFLUX Initiative has grown over the past four years, so has Scottsdale Public Art. The organization addresses new programming needs based on the changing economy and the role of public art in supporting tourism initiatives. The organization also increasingly focuses on temporary installations as a creative tool in place making. These installations are no longer an occasional random addition but rather pivotal elements of the program's broadening scope and value.

Waterfront District

The Scottsdale waterfront is a uniquely designed area that turned dirt pathways along the Arizona Canal into a vibrant, public space that has enlivened downtown by becoming a location for festivals and public art installations. The City of Scottsdale's contribution amounted to millions of dollars. Private development resulted in high-end condominiums, boutique shopping, and upscale restaurants. Working with Salt River Project (SRP), the entity that oversees all 131 miles of canals throughout the valley, the city has added an integral bicycle and pedestrian loop, which now draws people to downtown Scottsdale. The Scottsdale waterfront is almost unparalleled in the car-driven desert metropolis of the Valley of the Sun.

The Waterfront District in Scottsdale, as the canal area is euphemistically called, plays up the fact that Scottsdale is the only city in the valley with a canal, the Arizona Canal, running throughout its downtown. The district is the result of the visionary planning on the part of city officials, who in the late 1980s looked at the canal and its dirt banks and saw what it could become with housing, entertainment, restaurants, walking, bicycling, as well as horse trails through the downtown area.[5]

This vision, taking nearly twenty years, became the reality of the Waterfront District. The City of Scottsdale invested millions of dollars of infrastructure and entered into a special license agreement with SRP. The district's special designation brought the attention of developers, resulting in housing in an area that had lacked sufficient housing. The public space that was achieved encourages public interaction through recreation and creating a place to see and hear water in the harsh desert environment as well as providing some solace from the intense sun and heat with lush landscaping.

Scottsdale Public Art saw the waterfront as a prime downtown area to activate with temporary installations very early. The first iteration of what would later become a public art event, Night Lights on the Canal, took place on one Thursday for three consecutive months—October, November, and December in 2009. The result was to spark a growing interest in and focus on the waterfront area of downtown Scottsdale. The series of installations offered an opportunity for local artists to develop interactive works that received encouraging feedback from the public. While limited in scale, the idea sparked what has become Scottsdale Public Art's showcase event—Canal Convergence: Water + Art + Light.

Canal Convergence is the result of several years of efforts of a public art program working with a public utility. The intent of the partnership was to build public awareness of one of this desert city's most precious assets—water. Scottsdale Public Art could not have undertaken its groundbreaking work of temporary installations in the Arizona Canal without the permitting and purview of SRP. This unique merging of interests and the recognition of the role a public art program can play in educating the public about the working canal system and the pivotal role it plays in all our lives, for those of us living in the desert, has been experimental in approach. The result over the past three years has had successes in building a dialogue about water, using public art and artist-designed workshops. This concept has not always been an easy one to define. SRP's support has been absolutely critical to Scottsdale Public Art, not only undertaking its programming of installations in and along the canal but also helping to expand the programming. This unique partnership has developed into a strong, mutually supportive and creative collaboration. It has also resulted in a unique artist/industry residency program between Scottsdale Public Art and SRP.

One key factor to this collaboration has been the mutual interest of engaging with the public. SRP sees the role of Scottsdale Public Art as critical to devising ways for the public to encounter and gain knowledge of the urban waterways. Public art has effectively engaged community through interactive events like "fish herding" a necessary part of cleaning the canals on a periodic basis. Scottsdale Public Art saw an opportunity for local artists to design ways for the public to understand the importance of the canals, why the fish must be moved, and the necessity of maintenance. Hence, *Art + Maintenance* was created. The public was part of the audience and walking along the canal banks while trained SRP maintenance crews slowly moved or "herded" the fish to an area for transportation to another stretch of canal. It was a unique Scottsdale experience, but one that clearly characterized the collaborative approaches and new thinking for both public art and a public utility.

COMMUNITY BUILDING

Engaging community has been the foundation of Scottsdale Public Art. From very early on, its participation in a forty-year community tradition, the Scottsdale Arts Festival, has been only one example of this engagement. Bringing people to a community event and encouraging participation has been a primary focus. All of the previous examples have built a tradition and an expectation of experiential art in the public realm bringing community together and encouraging dialogue about public art.

Engaging community in an urban setting, and particularly in a southwestern city can seem daunting. Without a central downtown or central gathering place for community, large spread-out cities in the Southwest face some particular challenges.

Scottsdale, Arizona, benefits from a far more integral and much smaller downtown area. Building on its history of an arts and culture city that has attracted artists, Scottsdale continues to focus on revitalizing an aging infrastructure of its downtown. Public art has been a key in developing a thriving and attractive downtown. Community engagement also includes bringing people together for a common experience—something so rare in a world of individual interactions through social media. Are we social? Of course we are! But what exactly does this mean?

CONCLUSION

Is Scottsdale Public Art building a new paradigm for art in the public realm? Is it developing best practices for artists and public artists who practice social engagement? I like to think that Scottsdale Public Art continues to lead not only in what we present to the public but also in how we present it through our social media and through our interactive and engaging website.

What was once simply a fully funded city program is now something bigger. In addressing the change from being capital-project dominated, Scottsdale Public Art has in many ways led the way for other public art programs. Through experimentation over the past six years, Scottsdale Public Art has pushed the aesthetic and cultural values of its community using temporary art, events, and exhibitions, performance art–based stories, interactive residencies, and conversations with artists to solidify its national reputation and standing.

All of this means that programming funding has had to expand beyond city funding. Jack Becker, publisher of *Public Art Review*, in his most recent note suggests this same idea: "We need to broaden the scope and increase the effectiveness of government-run public art programs."[6] Becker's suggestion of supporting at the grassroots level the work of artists who are connected instinctively to community is important. But the concept of funding through private and other government and foundation sources to support public art dedicated to enervating and inspiring a community is the key. With private funding through corporate sponsorships, foundation and community grants, and increasing the monetary obligations of its advisory board, Scottsdale Public Art has gained the freedom to explore and design new and creative initiatives that reach out to the community, embed local artists, encourage national and international artists to bring installations, and to enable Scottsdale Public Art to commission installations. All of this is done with the community in mind.

Scottsdale as a city is very close to being landlocked. Any new capital projects resulting from any new bond funds will enable the city to complete roadways and its last fire station in the northern part of the city. Scottsdale Public Art, through its vibrant program of temporary installations, can continue to bring new and noteworthy artists to the community and build greater awareness of public art and its important and critical impact. And we can continue to engage the community in our work and our programs, because installations are changing, new exhibits continue to populate The Gallery @ the Library, and Canal Convergence continues to elevate the quality of public art.

Community building is judged not only in the numbers of public reached but also in the quality of the experience. In this respect, Scottsdale Public Art works tirelessly to engage community and to work with artists in noteworthy ways. Finding that balance, as Glenn Weiss points out in his article, "Art with Story,"[7] is where a public art event that draws crowds still has the quality of experience and the ability to touch and educate.

Scottsdale Public Art has utilized an outside public relations firm for the past two years expressly to focus on building awareness of its programming, getting air time on both radio and television as well as local, regional, and national coverage of its installations and Canal Convergence signature event. Is this necessary? The public relations aspect has been key to the success of Scottsdale Public Art's programming. Public relations bring the public to where we are. Then once they are there, it is our job to engage with them as a program and encourage visiting artists to interact with the public. As surveys continue to show, visitors are coming to Scottsdale for experiences with public art. Both marketing and surveys are powerful tools that have begun to help Scottsdale Public Art to quantify not only the numbers but the visitor experience.

Public art as a discipline does have a responsibility to engage the community in dialogue. It is critical that some visceral experience results from a public art experience, something that truly draws people to confront their own ideas or preconceived concepts. There are artists today working in social practice who push these boundaries. Gregory Sales's work in bringing social practice to his art may have started with *Love Buttons* in 2008 but has evolved to working with prisoners who use art to tell their stories. Candy Chang was commissioned for a temporary project with Scottsdale Public Art. Her practice requires opinions of her viewers. Her sticker project, *Public Art Is* . . . was commissioned by Scottsdale Public Art for the Public Art Network conference in San Diego in June 2012. Community is created through issues of shared concern, and how we connect invariably helps us recognize our shared values of community.

The experience is not only passive. As Kieran Long, curator at the Victoria and Albert Museum, recently suggested in an interview, engaging people in multisensory ways is important, and "we need to become a department of public life."[8] Community engagement, by its very nature, is active social practice. Public art provides possibilities for interaction, which can be found in few other venues or disciplines—it is an important and valued part of public life. Scottsdale Public Art continues to experiment and explore with its role as an urban public art program and its commitment to community engagement.

NOTES

1. City of Scottsdale, Arizona, Ordinance No. 3781, dated 1985; revised January 14, 1991, and May 20, 2008.

2. Scottsdale Public Art Master Plan 2012.

3. Kurt Perschke, "Temporary Art," Scottsdale Public Art website, 2008, http://www.scottsdalepublicart.org/temporary-art/redball.

4. Ibid.

5. *ArtScape: A Public Art Plan for Scottsdale,* Betty Drake for Scottsdale Cultural Council, July 1990.

6. Jack Becker, "A Wide Umbrella," Publisher's Note, *Public Art Review* 51 (Fall/Winter 2015): p. 13.

7. Glenn Weiss, "Art with Story," *Public Art Review* 51 (Fall/Winter 2015): 31.

8. Quoted in Edwin Heathcote, "New Homes for (Almost) Everything," *London Financial Times*, Section Collecting, September 17, 2014, 4.

4

City of Austin Art in Public Places Program

Jean Graham, Carrie Brown, Susan Lambe, and Meghan Wells

INTRODUCTION

This chapter highlights four public art projects commissioned through the Austin Art in Public Places (AIPP) program that were completed between 2010 and 2014 and feature vital components of community involvement. Each project has a unique social and physical context, and each represents a different strategy or process for successfully interfacing with the community. *Open Room Austin* is a functional and iconic place—an exaggerated domestic table-setting sited in an urban green space adjacent to a burgeoning downtown redevelopment. As intended by the artists, it is an urban stage. Its meaning continues to be reshaped, day and night, as Austinites invent ways to interact with it. Lit at night and sited on a hill that is easily visible to cars passing by along a downtown thoroughfare, it is a domestic icon inviting all to come participate. The locus of public involvement with this piece occurred not during the planning process but after the work was constructed and installed.

On the other hand, the sculptural installation *Uprooted Dreams* was conceived and created through a conceptual and actual hands-on collaboration with a targeted group of stakeholders—Austin's Latino immigrant population. It was commissioned for the Emma S. Barrientos Mexican American Cultural Center located in a historically Latino, recently gentrified neighborhood. The selected artist approaches her public art discipline as social practice and intended that an integral part of this artwork would be to create a safe context for empowered dialogue, with the social goal of enhancing cultural identity for its participants. After installation of the completed sculptures, the experience of collaboration remained in the memory of the participants, in their ongoing relationships and their transformed sense of identity. The general public can witness this collaborative experience of creation through two films and a published catalogue that document the workshop process.

45

The North Austin Community Garden, located at the North Austin YMCA, is the result of a public/private partnership whose goal was to create AIPP's first artist-designed community garden for an internationally diverse, affordable, outlying neighborhood. The idea for a community garden sprang from an existing partnership between the City of Austin and the YMCA and was contingent on a neighborhood group organizing to support the ongoing life of the project, which was to continue after the garden was constructed. From design development to the creation of bylaws to transfer ongoing responsibility to a garden leadership group, the project demanded cohesive community involvement and support. The artists designed the garden itself as well as a master plan for future development. In addition, the artists were an integral part of the creation of the social structures needed to support it.

Finally, the Barton Spring Pool project is located at a beloved iconic natural site close to the heart of many Austinites. Because this natural site itself is so central to Austin's sense of place and identity, a successful project required a delicate and sometimes turbulent process of collaboration to ensure the support of stakeholders. The design development was delayed and redirected, as passionate members of the public, protective of the site, strongly advocated for disparate points of view. After many revisions and relocations, the artist designed an artwork that successfully met the requirements of the community and the site and added value without disrupting the integrity of a beloved place.

AUSTIN ART IN PUBLIC PLACES (AIPP)

The City of Austin percent-for-art program began in 1985 with the passing of the AIPP ordinance.[1] Austin was the first municipality in Texas to make a commitment to include works of art in city construction projects. In 2002, the ordinance was amended to increase public art allocations from 1 to 2 percent of eligible construction budgets and to include the eligibility of streetscape projects, thus supporting greater visibility of art in the urban environment. Also in that year, the AIPP program was moved from the Parks and Recreation Department into the Economic Development Department.[2] In 2015, after thirty years of operation, the program has commissioned for the city's public art collection more than two hundred artworks, many of which have included active components of community participation. While the AIPP ordinance and guidelines do not outline specific requirements for community engagement, program leaders have always interpreted community buy-in and engagement as a mark of success for a project.[3]

SHAPING PUBLIC ENGAGEMENT

In the development of a public art project, there are several phases during which city administrators can choreograph successful public engagement. The development of the public art goals and the project outline is overarching at the onset of the project. In Austin, percent-for-art program funds for artwork become available through citizen-approved and city council–approved capital improvement projects (CIPs). AIPP project managers work with city departments, their contracted design consultants, and relevant community stakeholder groups to develop appropriate parameters for the project. These in turn must be approved by the AIPP Panel (a seven-member citizen oversight panel composed of arts professionals) and the Arts Commission (a citizen board whose members are appointed by city council).[4] The parameters outline the required qualifications of the artist, type of artwork appropriate for the site, any required community engagement process, and potential appropriately qualified members of the selection panel, which will have the deciding votes in the commission of an artist. Also outlined are the project advisors, who may be city staff, design consultants, technical experts, or community members. A description of the facility and any relevant history is provided along with information on the corresponding construction project. Fundamental project goals set in this project outline allow for varying degrees of artistic interpretation on the part of the artist.

The AIPP project manager uses this project outline as a guide to problem solve the processes and issues that may arise during the course of a project. What types of community input are called for? Where do you set boundaries to protect the integrity of the artist's vision? How do you take risks and relinquish control to allow the spontaneous development of true community building? How do you guide the artist in his/her communication with the public? The way these issues get addressed is unique to each project.

OPEN ROOM AUSTIN: SETTING THE STAGE

The Seaholm District

Austin is in the midst of transforming a portion of its urban core, on the southwest edge of downtown along the Colorado River (renamed Lady Bird Lake), that is anchored by the decommissioned Art Deco–style Seaholm Power Plant, which was built in the 1950s. After years of considering multiple ideas for the restoration and adaptive reuse of the site, Austin City Council approved the Seaholm District master plan to guide the comprehensive development of the area.[5] The Seaholm District is intended as a leading example of a multimodal, urban mixed-use and green development with advanced sustainable features. When completed, the district will feature office space, contemporary condos, retail shops, restaurants, a Trader Joe's market, public art, an outdoor terrace overlooking Lady Bird Lake, and an underground garage with a green-roof plaza. Shoal Creek, one of Austin's natural jewels, will be restored and will connect the site with Austin's network of greenbelts. East of the power plant and scheduled to open in 2016 will be Austin's new central public library, designed as a high-tech cultural and information center for the community.

To lay the groundwork and infrastructure for this landmark district, adjacent private properties began their own transformations. The City of Austin partnered with Gables Residential (located west of the power plant) to provide several public amenities, including a safe way for pedestrians to cross a busy Cesar Chavez Street, connection of private residences to the Seaholm District, construction of private commercial space, construction of three-quarters of an acre of new parkland with a storm water biofiltration pond, and connection to the crosstown Lance Armstrong Bikeway. As part of its development project, Gables Residential implemented the road and park improvements, managed the design and construction on the city's behalf, and provided a match of up to $100,000 to the eligible 2 percent AIPP funds for public art. This netted $200,000 for an artwork to be located on the new parkland, named Sand Beach Park.

Artist Involvement and Artwork Design Process

Through a competitive call to artists, the AIPP program selected the Miami-based artist team of R & R Studios, composed of Roberto Behar and Rosario Marquardt. In 2007, their design work began for what became *Open Room Austin*, the artwork to be installed in this new urban setting. AIPP encourages a collaborative approach that combines input and feedback from project stakeholders within the framework of artistic vision. In this private/public partnership, the process included dialogue with the developers to help inform the artwork design, facilitate integration, and meet the overall project goals.

In the case of *Open Room Austin*, the formative stages of participatory input were limited by the fact that the area's stakeholders were as yet unidentified. Because Gables Residential had not finished construction of its condominiums and retail spaces, it was unclear how added usage of the nearby pedestrian bridge would affect recreational and commuter use and traffic patterns; similarly, Seaholm's pedestrian and vehicular pathways and connections had not yet been confirmed. While the artists worked closely with Gables and the city project team, their siting and design of the work were largely based on educated guesses as to how the artwork might function in this new setting.

The artists moved forward with the clear goal of creating an artistic intervention that would address the stated artwork goals to (1) create a permanent, durable, and sustainable artwork that would withstand outdoor environmental elements; (2) create a work that responded to the vitality of the site, including the diverse modes of transportation for pedestrian, automotive, bicycle, and train; and (3) enhance an area of development and encourage use of the site by Austin citizens, Gables residents, and visitors.

An Artwork Emerges

Behar and Marquardt visited Austin several times to engage with the project team developing the site. During these visits, the artists absorbed planned mobility strategies and urban design priorities, became familiar with Austin's diverse population and unique civic personality, examined the plans for future urban development, and brainstormed artistic solutions that might best integrate with all of these aspects. This interconnected and complex set of factors informed the artists' design approach and allowed for a robust discussion of a variety of ideas as to how an artwork might function in the space and serve a diverse population.

The concept of *Open Room Austin* emerged from this design process and suggested a new way of providing interaction, place making, and social construction through an artistic platform. The artists proposed a social sculpture: an exaggerated domestic table setting sited in this urban green space that would allow for flexible usage to activate a core concept of bringing together a variety of the community in constantly changing ways. They intended the artwork's meaning to be reshaped as Austinites invent and explore ways to interact with it. It became clear that the broadest public participation would be provided *after* the work was installed, which would be a critical component of its function and success. This was in contrast to the traditional process of public participation and stakeholder input being most leveraged during the design phase.

The artists believed that it was important to provide a way to shift from "public" to "personal" in this public space. They wanted the piece to be seen as a beautiful addition to Austin's built environment but, perhaps more important, to serve as a stimulus for public interaction. To accomplish this, they focused on dichotomies: creating intimacy within a public setting and transforming "the familiar into the fantastic."[6] Their artwork bridges the world of popular culture with contemporary art in a way that resonates differently with each viewer, allowing for multiple meanings and various forms of encounters to be shaped through the same physical framework.

Open Room Austin was approved and installed in 2010 as an intimate "room"— a twenty-four-foot-long table and benches surrounded by four oversized living room lamps and a phalanx of crepe myrtles that, with growth over time, will lend an even greater physical and emotional sense of privacy. The table, digitally designed and constructed of powder-coated CNC-routed aluminum, is "covered" by a seemingly delicate lace tablecloth reminiscent of a grandmother's comfortable dining room. The oversized lamps, which shine a soft light onto the table starting at dusk, allow the room to be used for early morning and nighttime gatherings.

An Active Social Sculpture, Now and in the Future

The public usage and interaction has taken the form of various individual and collective events, encounters, and activities It has been the backdrop for engagement and bridal photos, birthday and myriad other celebrations; a resting spot for those traversing the Ann and Roy Butler Hike and Bike Trail that surrounds Lady Bird Lake; a site for dog meet-and-greets; a vantage point for thousands of sunsets and sunrises to be experienced privately or en masse; a setting for discussions, forums, salons, and the impromptu forging of friendships—for the moment or for longer.

Figure 4.1. OpenRoomAustin.
Photo by Philip Rogers

It has even inspired a citizen-generated Facebook profile that invites people to become "friends" with it—and many have responded. The artwork received a Best of 2010 honor from the local newspaper, the *Austin Chronicle*, when it was named the "Best Place to Table-Dance at a Family Reunion." The newspaper described it as "a fun, adult-friendly design playground" to the glee of a partying public.[7] The city's public art collection manager was less enthusiastic about the newspaper's encouraging people to dance on the table and later had to oversee the repair of damage that occurred as a result of such activity.

Open Room Austin continues to serve visitors to Sand Beach Park in its unassuming and relatable concept, with more and more public programming and spontaneous interventions. In the years to come, its function within the context of the completed Seaholm District may generate new uses by an even broader segment of the population but in ways that remain true to the artists' intent of providing experiential meaning through diverse interaction with this public art piece. This artwork along with others that provide a platform for engagement and interaction provide a springboard for public artists and public art programs to open the door to ideas that go beyond a static sculpture or mural. Cities that embrace these new artistic interventions are expanding the definition of "public art" and allowing for community identity to emerge in new ways. It is a creative risk but one that is calculated to broaden citizens' experience with their surroundings and bring new, dynamic layers of meaning to public spaces.

UPROOTED DREAMS:
PUBLIC ART AS COMMUNITY PRACTICE

The idea of establishing a Mexican American–focused cultural facility in Austin was first promoted in the 1970s by Latino artists and activists. After many years of continued advocacy by community members and elected officials, the Austin City Council initiated a task force in 1986 and two years later commissioned a feasibility study to explore this possibility. Finally, in 1999, after a failed attempt in 1992, the citizens of Austin approved funding for a Mexican American cultural arts facility to be located on six acres in downtown Austin along Lady Bird Lake. Teodoro Gonzales de Leon, a Mexican architect, was chosen to be the lead architect. Due to budget constraints, the project was designed to be built in phases. The first phase of the Emma S. Barrientos Mexican American Cultural Center (ESB-MACC) was completed and opened to the public in September 2007.

Public Artwork for the ESB-MACC

As part of the initial construction, the AIPP program commissioned artist Benito Huerta to design *Snake Path*, an eight-hundred-foot walkway composed of colored pavers that transects the site. The sidewalk's red-yellow-black pattern references the Mexican milk snake, which thrives on both sides of the Mexico-U.S. border. Later, when an additional 2 percent funds became available to AIPP in conjunction with construction of an education wing, the chosen direction was to commission an artist to design a shade structure for the open plaza, or *zocalo*. The ESB-MACC Advisory Board, which oversees the operation of the facility, strongly advocated for a community-based artwork, partly as a way to encourage community connection with the new facility. In response to that desire and with the support of the AIPP Panel, AIPP solicited an artist to create a permanent artwork that would visually and artistically enhance the vestibule of the new education wing and deepen visitors' understanding of the center's educational and cultural mission to preserve, create, present, and promote Mexican American cultural arts and heritage.

The request for qualifications stressed community engagement without dictating to the artist how that should be interpreted. The five-member voting selection panel included two Latino artists, a design professional who was also an ESB-MACC community advisory board member, a curator who was also an AIPP panel member, and an independent curator. This group was guided by advisors, including program staff from the ESB-MACC and the city parks department, the city project manager for the construction of the building, a representative from the architecture firm, and another member of the ESB-MACC Advisory Board. After deliberations and interviews, the selection panel and advisors chose to commission Margarita Cabrera, a first-time public artist from El Paso, Texas, whose studio work addresses socioeconomic issues along the U.S.-Mexico border. Her artistic practice had already taken the format of participatory workshops designed to resist the disappearance of cultural roots and engage individuals with little or no voice within the established art world.

Process of Collaboration: Building Community

Cabrera began by meeting with Austin Latino individuals and groups with the goal of initiating dialogue about issues facing their communities. These discussions informed the artistic direction of her project. The subjects of being uprooted and gentrification were ubiquitous in these conversations. Many of the historic Latino neighborhoods located east of Interstate 35 and adjacent to the ESB-MACC had transformed during the preceding decade from areas populated by small single-family homes to trendy bar districts filled with high-rise condos. This transformation resulted in skyrocketing land valuations, which served to threaten community cohesion and the sense of belonging of long-term residents.

Settling on the title *Uprooted Dreams*, Cabrera chose to collaborate with a group from Austin's Mexican American immigrant community in the creation of an artwork installation for the education vestibule. She invited two master artisans from Oaxaca, Mexico, Ranulfo Sergio Ibañes and Lucia Luria Sosa, who work in the *alebrije* wood-carving tradition, to share their skills and cultural heritage with the participants. The group met together in a month-long series of hands-on workshops at the ESB-MACC, creating a series of sculptures informed by this Oaxacan artisan tradition.

First, participants collected wood in a neighborhood park of long-term significance to Austin's Latino community, and a dance group was invited to perform a ceremonial acknowledgment of the earth in accordance with Aztec tradition. Then they worked together in the process of carving, sanding, connecting, and painting wood sculptures, each person transforming tree limbs and branches into a unique shape that portrayed an individual experience of uprootedness. In the process, they shared personal experiences and formed a trusting creative community that acknowledged and encouraged each other's individual stories and talents. Cabrera invited all participants to engage directly in the creative process of the workshop and respected all of them as cocreators. She provided an unprecedented public platform for a self-reflective creative process to individuals who had not previously experienced this kind of opportunity.

Lasting Impact

The resulting site-specific sculptural installation, *Uprooted Dreams*, features more than nineteen brightly colored carvings grouped in a unified installation along the walls and ceiling at the entrance of the education area at the ESB-MACC. The work imparts a strong visual impact on those who enter and brings vitality to the geometrically strong, stark architecture. As part of her commission and in order to leverage the educational potential of the project, Cabrera documented the workshop process with a printed catalogue that included a curatorial essay and two films, one

Figure 4.2. UprootedDreams.
Photo by Jean Graham

documenting the *alebrije* artisans in Oaxaca and the other documenting the collaborative human experience of the participant creators.[8] These remain available to the public at the ESB-MACC and at the Austin Public Library.

Cabrera's objective for the *Uprooted Dreams* project was as much to create a safe space for community dialogue and affirmation as it was to establish a lasting, successful site-specific art installation. The project was successful in both regards, without one aspect compromising the other. AIPP and ESB-MACC staff worked together to resolve uncharted issues having to do with an extended group residency, such as child care, space usage, safety and scheduling. The project became a model for an ongoing Latino Arts Residence Program developed later by the ESB-MACC for Latino arts organizations and artists in all disciplines. Through this project, Cabrera activated the concept of public art as a social practice and moved the element of community participation in public art into a more conceptually grounded and political realm.

NORTH AUSTIN COMMUNITY GARDEN: SUSTAINABLE ART

A Public-Private Partnership

In 2011, AIPP staff began discussing artwork opportunities for a new recreation center being built to replace an aging YMCA in one of Austin's very diverse northern neighborhoods, located nine miles from downtown. The recreation center was built as a public/private partnership between the City of Austin and the YMCA of Austin. This unique partnership proved to be a key element in the success of what would become Austin's first artist-designed community garden.

The residents of the surrounding neighborhood had long advocated for a larger and more accessible facility for its growing yet underserved community. Their persistent advocacy included the desire for outdoor gathering spaces and a community garden. During the design development of the facility, a local architectural firm, Studio8, spent much time working with residents to merge their expectations with the goals of the city and the YMCA. One result of that effort was the inclusion of a community garden in the site plan. Unfortunately, the available budget did not include funds to implement the garden, so it remained as a placeholder.

Garden Design as Public Art

Due to staff shortages, AIPP did not begin working on this project until the design of the facility was well established, resulting in a timeframe that limited opportunities to integrate artwork into the design. This missed opportunity became the catalyst for the creative brainstorming that gave staff the opportunity to propose a bold new idea: hire an artist to build the community garden that neighbors so desperately wanted. Fortunately, the project partners—Studio8, the YMCA, and city staff—were excited about this idea and were willing to be trailblazers in this venture.

The artwork opportunity then needed clarification. Would AIPP commission an artist to design a fence around the garden or a sculpture in the garden, or would the entire garden be within the design scope of an artist? After numerous discussions that explored many options, the project team and the AIPP Panel agreed to the latter. AIPP would commission an artist to design and build a community garden, placing considerable emphasis on community engagement.

Working with the project team, which now included staff from the Sustainable Food Center, a local nonprofit in partnership with the YMCA, and the newly formed Sustainable Urban Agriculture and Community Garden Program of the city's Parks and Recreation Department, AIPP staff developed the public art goals for the project. They were to (1) integrate the perspective of an artist in the design and cultivation of a community garden; (2) create a gathering space maintained and enjoyed by diverse neighbors that engenders stewardship and a shared sense of pride in community; (3) produce a functioning and sustainable garden that yields fresh produce for the community; (4) open the artistic process to the community through workshops and public events; and (5) reflect on the concept of health for "mind, spirit, and body" through innovative expressions of visual art in a garden setting.

However, important questions remained. What type of artist would be solicited? What guidelines would be used to review applications? What questions would be asked during the finalist interviews? Was it possible to find an artist with all of the skills required? Despite all of these questions, AIPP staff was confident that the knowledge and resources of the project team would compensate in areas where the artist might be lacking. This provided the selection panel with the flexibility to consider a wide variety of skill sets.

Artists and Community Engagement

After a competitive selection process, AIPP commissioned artists/architects Lucy Begg and Robert Gay, a husband-and-wife team who directs an Austin-based design studio. The artists quickly began meeting with the project team and developing a community engagement strategy. It was decided that the artists would spend nearly 10 percent of their budget on community engagement activities, much more than the typical AIPP project. This proved to be a critical decision.

During the course of the project, the artists worked extensively with the local community through workshops and public events to develop the design of the garden. This allowed residents to have a direct impact on decisions such as what types of beds were installed, where water hoses would be located, and whether or not there would be composting on site. Outreach activities included information booths at multiple public events hosted by the YMCA, presentations to various community groups, online surveys and blogs, design charrettes, and participating in community garden leadership classes presented by the Sustainable Food Center at the YMCA. In addition, the artists held three community participation days during the garden's construction: one day to build the fence, another to build the garden beds, and the last to prepare the garden for the public opening. Participants were aided by volunteers from J. E. Dunn Construction, the company that built the facility. The artists also established the Garden Leadership Group (which would eventually be led by community volunteers) to develop a governing structure and bylaws, including membership rules and fees. This infrastructure allowed for a smooth transition of authority after the artists' work was completed and the keys to the gate were literally handed over to the community.

Challenges and Successes

When reservations for the garden plots became available, the majority of the forty-eight available plots were reserved within the first four hours. This was the first true reading of the success of this project. During the artists' design phase, a major obstacle arose on submission of the permit application. A portion of the garden was located in the one-hundred-year flood plain, which severely restricted what could be built there and what could be done to the soil. Instead of drastically changing the garden design after receiving this news, the project team decided to relocate the garden out of the flood plain and into a larger area at the edge of the property. This change provided the artists with an opportunity to double the size of the garden, though their budget did not increase. With the foresight and encouragement of the YMCA, the artists created a master plan for the entire site; the first phase would be built with the public art budget and the second would be built after funds could be raised by the YMCA and the Garden Leadership Group. This commitment to the future was another sign of the project's success. At the end of the project, the artists created a final report, which documented the community engagement strategies that were utilized and provided lessons learned and recommendations for implementation of phase 2. The report highlighted the successful outcome of the formalized partnerships and the investment of time and money in small-group and one-on-one engagement with the community. The report also recommended a thorough investigation of the environmental conditions of a site before commencing design to avoid delays in the permitting process.

Artwork Dedication—with Vegetables

On May 17, 2014, the North Austin Community Garden officially opened to the public. Vegetables were abundant, as gardeners had already been using their plots for two months. A local Girl Scout troop built a lending library to make books about gardening accessible. By the time the garden opened, a square-foot gardening class was being offered, and more were added within the following year. In addition, a fifteen-minute documentary film titled *GARDEN*, created by a local production company that had followed the entire project, was presented to an enthusiastic audience.[9] From the beginning, all parties had agreed that documentation would be a vital educational component, and the support and resources of the YMCA made possible a powerful and lasting film about this truly innovative project. The collaboration was successful in fostering much neighborhood pride and stimulating the creation of community in this North Austin neighborhood. The project was not without obstacles, but in the end it succeeded largely due to the dedicated partners involved, including the artists.

BARTON SPRINGS POOL:
ENGAGING WITH A CULTURAL ICON

To understand how the Barton Springs Pool public art project's civic engagement process unfolded, it is important to understand the cultural importance of Barton Springs to the City of Austin. Barton Springs is an expansive, icy-cold natural-spring pool locally acknowledged as the very soul of Austin. Set in a verdant park shaded by old pecan trees, the pool, combined with the people and the place, creates a cultural mecca that Austinites are proud to point to as *most revered* in a city full of beloved cultural touchstones. Barton Springs, actually a group of four springs, are artesian springs issuing under pressure from a fault line in the underlying limestone formation. Locals celebrate the surrounding flora and the fauna, most especially the Barton Springs salamander, which exists nowhere else in the world. Due to steady stewardship by the Austin Parks and Recreation Department (PARD), the Texas Commission on Environmental Quality, and the U.S. Fish and Wildlife Service, people from all over the world have been able to enjoy the swimming in the sixty-eight-degree waters while the resident endangered salamander continues to thrive.

Historical Significance of the Site

Long before Barton Springs Pool's current popularity, the natural springs were considered sacred and the site was used as a reliable and comfortable campsite by various Native American tribes who inhabited the area. In the 1730s, Spanish Franciscan friars built a mission there, and eventually Anglo colonists began settling the area. In 1937, "Uncle Billy Barton" purchased what was called Spring Creek and eventually promoted the site as a tourist attraction and swimming hole. Andrew Jackson Zilker was the last private owner of the property, and in 1917, the City of Austin purchased fifty acres of land to be designated as a public park.

Stewardship of Barton Springs

Once the city acquired Barton Springs, the long process of responsible public stewardship began. Over the years, Austin City Council has passed several ordinances to protect Barton Springs, including a citizen-initiated Save Our Springs Ordinance designed in 1992 to limit development in the Edwards Aquifer Recharge Zone and protect water quality.[10] Barton Springs was designated as a City of Austin Historic Landmark in 1990, and seven years later, the Zilker Park Historic District was listed on the National Register of Historic Places.

Later, the city recognized that maintenance and improvements to Barton Springs Pool were overdue. In 2009, Austin City Council adopted the *Barton Springs Pool Master Plan: Concepts for Preservation and Improvement,* which was developed through an extensive three-year public process that included over eighty public meetings, four town-hall meetings, and the receipt of voluminous input from stakeholders.[11]

The city council approved funding for some of the improvements to be completed within a five-year period. Grounds improvements in support of the master plan included modifying public spaces to create healthier root structures for trees; improving drainage and diverting nonpoint source pollution; adding more accessible paths for people, including those with mobility impairments; and creating improved multimodal parking.

Public Art Commission: The Public Defines the Opportunity

The AIPP-eligible funds for this Barton Springs Capital Improvement Project (CIP) netted a modest $26,500 budget to commission an artwork. When AIPP staff research revealed the master plan–identified need for seating in the area, one of the project goals became to create multiple works of art that serve as seating strategies for site visitors. The other goals identified in the request for qualifications were for the artist to create a unique work of contemporary art for the public; consider the use, history, and cultural significance of the site; and create a work of art that was easily maintained and safe.

From the group of applicants, the selection panel recommended artist/artisan and native Austinite Hawkeye Glenn for the commission. The panel made the selection based on his design and fabrication ability, sensitivity to context, and use of indigenous pecan and limestone. As it turned out, these qualities, particularly the sensitivity to context, were crucial to the project's eventual success.

With a carefully selected artist for the site, the AIPP project manager and the artist began to engage the public in a dialogue regarding the artwork opportunity in order to determine how the artwork would be integrated into the site. The CIP was overseen on a monthly basis by a special joint committee of the city's parks board and the environmental board. The first joint committee meeting that the artist attended was an opportunity for him to listen to the public discourse regarding the planned site improvements. This meeting clarified that the CIP was under great public scrutiny, with many vocal citizens opposing any and every proposed site improvement. Differing factions were at work, some adamant that there be no change to the park, and some willing to be convinced that changes may be needed but making clear that each change would be scrutinized closely. The trust between the public and the city at this point appeared to be strained.

At the next meeting, the AIPP project manager briefed the committee on the artist selection process, and Glenn shared his initial thoughts regarding possible materials for the artwork. While citizens attending the meeting questioned the selection process, they seemed to embrace the artist himself, who had pointed to his long personal history with Barton Springs. Subsequently, the artist returned to the joint committee with initial thoughts regarding his design, which were simple forms rendered in native limestone embedded into the terrain just south of the springs, under existing trees for shade, and inside the fence defining the pool area. The rancor the public was feeling for the planned disturbances of the land within the fenced area was directed toward the artist when he proposed installing his work in environmentally sensitive areas. The artist met many times with the joint committee and with PARD staff, who strongly suggested that he remove his artwork to outside the drip line of any existing trees for the health of the trees and to satisfy public sentiment. Despite this pressure, the artist felt the integrity of his concept required that his proposed location remain unchanged.

In the end, staff directed the artist to place the artwork outside the drip line of any existing trees and outside the south gate of the pool perimeter. This new location helped restore public trust and was in accordance with the Barton Springs master plan. The artist accepted the new location with good will and prepared to begin his design for the new site. However, at that point, PARD staff requested that AIPP place a hold on the artist's work until the heated public process regarding the CIP site improvements was completed. Ultimately, this delay added two years to the project timeline. Throughout the project timeline, City of Austin staff spent hundreds of hours gathering input from the public and incorporating this community wisdom into the final iteration of the master plan, which ultimately created site improvements that are truly of and for the people. The city government and its citizens were both deeply committed to the public engagement process, even when collaboration became contentious. The pool, the setting, and the public art ultimately benefitted from this.

Interactive Public Listening

Once the artist was cleared to begin design again, the AIPP project manager proposed a four-day, on-site interactive public listening session and publicized the hours when the artist would be present to listen to the public. Additionally, an eight-by-twenty-foot white vinyl canvas (recycled billboard material) was installed at Barton Springs with an abundant supply of markers to allow the public to make comments at any time. Many site users commented on what sort of art would be best for the site, while others questioned the need for any artwork at all, writing opinions such as "Art is bad" and "The spring *IS* the art."

After this event, and with the promise that the artwork would be placed outside the pool fence, the public contentiousness abated. Glenn created an artwork that fulfilled the goals of the project and added an interactive element that speaks directly to Barton Springs as the soul of Austin. His piece, titled *Prayer Wheel*, is a limestone bench capable of accommodating six to eight people. Mounted at the end of the bench is a porcelain enameled steel orb that the visitors can spin. Colored in shades of blue, green, and beige, the orb resembles a drop of water. The idea for this component came to the artist after the listening event.

CONCLUSION

These four projects commissioned by the City of Austin AIPP program demonstrate a range of strategies for engaging the public in public art and stimulating the creation and ongoing experience of community for citizens. *Open Room Austin* set an iconic stage for people and provided a domestic site for ongoing social interactions in an urbanized environment. *Uprooted Dreams* was the most intensely collaborative during the design and fabrication process—challenging a targeted immigrant population to create community and self-identity through the creation of enduring public art. The North Austin Community Garden also provided a context for a community-building, sustainable activity to have an ongoing life. In addition, the artists collaborated with citizens in the actual design of the social structures needed to support this physical structure and activity. *Prayer Wheel* was developed for a well-loved site through a long process of civic engagement that, though often contentious, resulted in the city, the artist, and the public working together for a successful outcome.

Each public art project inevitably presents unique challenges, and care must be taken by the administrator to assess the resources available, respond to the entire context and parameters of each project, and remain flexible and open-ended in one's approach. Community engagement can come at different times in the process and can take different forms. Artists possess a wide range of skill sets, and it is important to set clear goals for a project through the solicitation and selection process. Ideally there will be a match between the commissioned artist and the project goals, but once the commission is underway, the artist's design or project expectations may need to evolve based on the conditions and skill set of those involved. Partnerships can be developed in a variety of ways, but it is important to set clear guidelines for these partnerships. On a practical level, it is important for the administrator to budget appropriately to include the time and resources necessary for public engagement to develop and support the project; this includes the artist's budget and staff time. In addition, funds for documentation are an important way to ensure ongoing education, empathy, and enthusiasm for the life of a project that is intended to live in the public realm for many years. Finally, expanding the notion of what art is and can be, may yield powerful and unexpected results. This requires that the administrator be willing to take educated risks, remain flexible, and avoid reverting to formulaic solutions.

NOTES

1. Code of the City of Austin, Texas, § 7–2: Art in Public Places, accessed January 22, 2015, https://www.municode.com/library/tx/austin/codes/code_of_ordinances.

2. The Economic Development Department "leads the global business recruitment, urban regeneration, small business development, cultural arts, and music efforts for the City of Austin." The move to this department provides AIPP opportunities to interact with private developers and civic leaders, encourages interdepartmental collaboration, and integration into the broad context of city planning ("Economic Development Department," Official Austin, Texas, website, accessed January 22, 2015, http://www.austintexas.gov/department/economic-development).

3. *AIPP Program Guidelines*, revised February 5, 2004, section II.A, accessed January 22, 2015, http://www.austintexas.gov/sites/default/files/files/aipp_guidelines.pdf.

4. Code of the City of Austin, § 2–1–103: Arts Commission, accessed January 22, 2015, https://www.municode.com/library/tx/austin/codes/code_of_ordinances?nodeId=TIT2AD_CH2-1CIBO_ART2BO_S2-1-103ARCO.

5. *Master Development Agreement between the City of Austin and Seaholm Power Development, LLC, Concerning the Redevelopment of the Seaholm Power Plant, Austin, Texas*, accessed January 22, 2015, http://www.austintexas.gov/sites/default/files/files/Redevelopment/Redevelopment_Projects/SeaholmMDA.pdf.

6. R+R Studios, "Open Room Austin," final design presentation, February 29, 2008.

7. "Best of Austin 2010 Critics' Picks," *Austin Chronicle*, http://www.austinchronicle.com/best-of-austin/year:2010/poll:critics/category:architecture-and-lodging/.

8. Art in Public Places, *Uprooted Dreams* (Austin: City of Austin, 2012); *Hand to Hand: Uprooted Dreams*, produced by Guillermo Monteforte, YouTube video, 16:33, posted by Nidia Holguin, October 22, 2013, https://www.youtube.com/watch?v=MmPWG2IqK0E; *Uprooted*

Dreams 2012—Margarita Cabrera, YouTube video, 9:45, posted by Nidia Holguin, September 9, 2013, https://www.youtube.com/watch?v=674p1axpEtc.

9. Flow Nonfiction, a local film production company, was hired by the YMCA to produce a short documentary about the project. The film premiered at the YMCA's annual meeting at the Stateside Theater in downtown Austin on May 14, 2014. At the event, AIPP received the Community Partner of the Year award for its participation in the North Austin Community Garden project.

10. Save Our Springs Initiative, Code of the City of Austin, Texas, § 30–5, Article 13 (passed January 15, 1992).

11. Austin City Council, Resolution 20090115-028 (passed January 15, 2009). A history of Barton Springs is given in *Barton Springs Pool Master Plan: Concepts for Preservation and Improvement* (2009), 25–51, accessed January 15, 2015, http://www.austintexas.gov/page/about-barton-springs-pool-master-plan.

5

Art and Civic Engagement

Collaboration Is Key

Robyn Vegas

INTRODUCTION

Imagine a world without art. It would be a somber existence to wake up to day after day. Art is the color and beauty of life, a reflection of ourselves, the stamp that says this is who we are as a culture. Comprehensive cultural arts programs and community engagement are as crucial in today's social order as they were historically. Communities must set art and culture as a high priority or else fail to deliver a basic component of any thriving society. It is the responsibility of government leaders, civic groups, business leaders, and decision makers as well as community members to work toward this common goal: art is not an elective; it is essential.

In this chapter I will describe some of the things local governments have done to develop and fund public art. As such it can serve as a sort of blueprint to government leaders who wish to expand their public art programs.

Public art and community involvement are key ways to engage people, strengthen civic commitment, and appeal to diverse populations. I've witnessed successful and not-so-successful attempts at this process. I believe the best way to achieve these goals is through creative collaborations with a variety of organizations or individuals. Good public art serves as a catalyst for municipal and economic development, raises the value and quality of life, defines an area, creates place making, and cultivates a sense of collective pride and ownership.

South Florida is known as a major tourist destination and for its beautiful beaches and nightlife. But the thriving art scene is just as integral a part of the vibrancy that is our trademark. According to the U.S. Census, Broward County has more than 1.8 million residents, 10,000 artists, 6,523 arts-related businesses that employ 23,497 people, 823 not-for-profit cultural organizations, and 31 cities, some of which operate their own arts councils and public art programs.[1] Neighboring counties Palm

Beach and Dade also boast impressive thriving arts offerings, which has led some to coin the tri-county area as the "Art Coast."

My background as an arts program coordinator for a nonprofit and municipal organizations has given me opportunities to facilitate and witness what I believe to be outstanding examples of utilizing the arts for community involvement. While the projects and programs are varied, the goal is always to use the arts as a communicator and catalyst for civic participation, for sharing arts information, and as a call to action to contribute to the improvement of the community and deeper aesthetic appreciation. The best civic engagement practices always have some level of partnerships, and a capacity for collaboration is essential. The projects and programs I will share are meant to inspire others to follow a similar model of cooperation and teamwork.

IMAGINATION SQUARED

Imagination Squared was a positive community-wide art response project that fulfilled the mission of art for the people, by the people. Dolf James and Christina Foard of Jacksonville, Florida, initiated the idea of *Imagination Squared: The Creative Response Experiment* during one of their monthly critique sessions. In James's studio, gessoed (usually wood) boxes were lying around for use in his sculpture. Ford suggested each artist who visited be encouraged to paint a box while chatting. The boxes were hung in a grid on the wall, and as it grew, it became more compelling. One thing led to another, and the decision was made to build hundreds of them and try and get a box into the hands of every artist in the Jacksonville area, creating a huge grid to hang in a public location. The result was a snapshot of Jacksonville's imagination. It was also part of a traveling exhibition around the city bringing widespread visibility to the project.[2]

The City of Pembroke Pines in Broward County, Florida, embraced the project and took it a step further by offering the squares to all levels of community participation: artists, business community members, city officials, students—basically anyone who wished to take part. The six-by-six-foot wood squares were distributed for several months and garnered the attention of many community members, from one-year-olds to ninety-five-year-olds. A one-dollar donation was suggested to help cover the cost of the cubes, which the municipal carpentry shop had built.

An important component of community engagement is to find creative ways to communicate with individuals outside of the art world and make them feel both welcomed into and encouraged in the creative process, to feel that their input is valid and that we hear their voices. A key to the success of the *Imagination Squared* project was a partnership with the Broward County Public Library system. They used their Summer Big Read program to advertise the project and serve as additional distribution sites along with city-run facilities for locals to obtain squares.

The response was overwhelming. *Imagination Squared* was an attractive draw both to local artists and beyond the normal "art scene," with participation by the community at large. Over five hundred six-by-six wooden squares were completed. The participants returned pieces to Studio 18, a city-run artists' studio work space and gallery, where they were hung as a permanent art "mosaic" reflecting the personal perspectives of the community members who participated.

Part of the joy of the project was hearing the deeply meaningful stories of each person who dropped off their art squares. A former ballerina, now in her nineties, reflected on the happiest time of her life and created a fabric square with ballet shoes. She said the project gave her a reason to be creative again and stirred up deep emotional feelings A middle-aged man said he had never created anything but felt compelled to write a message on his square about life and love, reflecting on the cancer his wife was battling. A local man wrapped his square in newspaper in a folded envelope pattern and shared that his grandmother had been too poor to have a purse and used to carry her money in a similarly folded newspaper. Her Alzheimer's had left her with few memories, but something was still alive inside her, much like the wooden square hidden inside the paper held something that was not easy to access but still existed.

When given an opportunity to express themselves, creativity flowed from many who did not identify themselves as "artists." This project proved that we all share a desire to be creative and express ourselves in unique ways. In the years that have followed the installation, returning visitors still come to the gallery, and it is a favored attraction where new patrons spend time discovering and enjoying the work.

THE COMMUNITY

Another public art installation, called *The Community*, was created by urban pop artist Ruben Ubiera. Ruben Ubiera is a Dominican neofigurative artist known for his strong use of the line. He paints and draws in a style considered by many as pop-surrealism, but he prefers to call it urban-pop, since he has lived most of his life in the urban, populated areas and most of his inspiration is derived from the interactivity between man and his urban environment. His background inspired the idea for *The Community* as a way to reflect on how every person is an important part of the total community.[3]

The artist had several brick towers constructed and permanently affixed outside of various buildings around the city. The four-sided cubes became a canvas for Ubiera to create portraits of locals. At an art festival, patrons were invited to get their photos taken as inspiration for the faces on the brick towers. Participants also submitted Facebook photos to the artist, and from among all the images, the artist chose four for each brick tower. The local arts and culture advisory board also embraced the project and helped pay for the cost of the materials. The vision of the project with the inclusion of the locals for inspiration was an excellent marriage of art and community. It was a natural fit to install the sculptures around the city where the artist's subject models lived and worked. The strong human element, with it's striking, bold aesthetic, appealed to passersby and created place making for the facilities it adorned.

Ubiera describes the project, which he had simmering in his mind for several years, as a symbol of how everyone in the community helps to build that place: "I believe 'The Community' touches part of my past and part of everyone's future. A building cannot be raised without a strong foundation, the same goes for a community. Brick by brick, everyone equally important. Stroke by stroke, let me shape my surrounds [*sic*] instead of my surroundings shaping me."[4]

Part of the success of *The Community* was the widespread appeal to the public to be part of the project via photo opportunities and encouraged buy-in to the concept. The final placement of the finished pieces for all to enjoy at art centers, parks, galleries, and recreation centers throughout the city created a sense of unity and familiarity with the art. Featuring a varied cross section of the pubic, ranging in different ages, races, and genders, appealed to a wide audience and celebrated diversity in our community.

Other ways to creatively engage can be fostered by using town meetings, public surveys, public hearings, charrettes, or workshops. When public arts projects are in the planning stages, distributing information at exhibits, music performances, festivals, churches, and in other community gatherings will prove fruitful. Moreover, investing time in these endeavors will strengthen public commitment and acceptance.

IMPACT OF ARTS ON THE ECONOMY

The economic impact of nonprofit arts and cultural activities in Broward County, as determined by Americans for the Arts, is $230 million annually. When broken down into spending by audiences and organizations, the nonprofit organizations spend $103 million each year, leveraging a remarkable $127 million in additional spending by arts and culture audiences.[5] This is vital revenue pumped into local restaurants, hotels, retail stores, parking garages, and other businesses.

The study, conducted in 2010, provides compelling evidence that the arts do mean business for the economy. These figures are important to note as further confirmation of why civic engagement and urban art should be supported in our communities: when the arts thrive, people want to live, work, and play in that area.

THE ARTS MEAN BUSINESS

Business for the Arts of Broward is a nonprofit organization that engages business leaders to advocate and educate about the importance of the county's art and cultural community as well as to recognize the connection between cultural vitality, creative success, and economic development. The nonprofit was formed by business leader Jarett Levan, with recommendation and support from the Broward County Cultural

Division, a local arts agency that provides financial, technical, and marketing assistance to artists and arts organizations.

Jarett Levan, chair of Business for the Arts of Broward, underscores the importance of arts organizations, saying they "have proven to be significant economic drivers for our community making supporting the arts good business. A call for greater community involvement and civic engagement is the responsibility of business leaders, elected officials, advocates, participants, artists and patrons."[6]

CULTURAL TOURS

One of the many inventive programs by Business for the Arts of Broward are the cultural tours. The tours were established to escort a select group of business executives on a guided, behind-the-scenes tour of some of the county's best cultural treasures. Partnering with the Broward County Cultural Division, the bimonthly tours are a unique way to expose the community to different art experiences and form new collaborations between the attendees and the arts organizations.

The tour is a daylong trip where attendees sample some of Broward's premier art and cultural destinations, such as ArtServe, the Bonnet House, Young at Art Museum, Museum of Art Fort Lauderdale, Broward Center for the Performing Arts, Museum of Discovery and Science, Sailboat Bend Artists' Lofts, the Art and Culture Center of Hollywood, Studio 18 in the Pines, African American Research Library, F.A.T. Village, and more.

"The tour was very informative and a really worthwhile way to spend a day!" said Nanette Saylor, one of the tour attendees. "It was a pleasure to get to do a deep dive into the organizations, and I was particularly impressed that we had the opportunity have the key players as our tour guides at each location."[7]

Juliet Roulhac, another attendee, describes it as "a day of art immersion," adding, "It was illuminating to realize that there is something for everyone in Broward— diverse art, theatre, and culture, it's all here for the taking and I would never have known it unless I went on the tour."[8]

The cultural tours are an example of how partnerships can benefit and increase a widespread audience and garner support for the arts community as a whole. The tours develop new voices for arts and culture in each group, who leave feeling inspired to further engage, volunteer, patronize, and become arts advocates. Using the tours as a springboard to educate the attendees about how the arts impact the community has proven an invaluable tool for recruiting support for the arts.

POWER2GIVE

In late 2010, the Arts and Science Council of Charlotte–Mecklenburg began development of power2give.org, a groundbreaking new website designed to address changing trends in philanthropic giving. The final product was a unique website that allows anyone to easily give a gift for the purpose of supporting specific projects or organizations they are most passionate about. With tools and resources for both donors and nonprofits, power2give makes posting projects, promoting them to different audiences, and giving to projects convenient for all involved.

In addition, Business for the Arts of Broward hosts a local power2give site (www. power2give.org/broward), which is designed to connect donors with projects they are passionate about. The site allows nonprofit organizations to post and promote arts and cultural projects in need of funding and invites donors to contribute directly to the projects that are most intriguing to them. The site launched in 2012, and in two years the Broward chapter raised over $474,300.00 on power2give and helped fund 94 projects.[9]

The projects Broward's power2give site has supported have focused on addressing various issues of public concern through use of the arts, including issues such as suicide; impoverished, abused, and at-risk youth; literacy; bullying; foster care; autism; AIDS; the elderly; nursing-home patients; cancer; hospice residents; Alzheimer's; the LGTB community; the disabled community; and many others.

Online giving, it turns out, is a great way to engage the community in the arts. It has proven to be a successful tool for arts and cultural participation; offers simple ways for posting, donating, and promoting projects; and is both convenient and engaging. In addition to funds raised online, the John S. and James L. Knight Foundation, the Broward County Cultural Division, the Community Foundation of Broward, BBX Capital, and other organizations have provided matching funds for projects on the site. These partnerships have been crucial to the success of the crowd source funding campaigns.

Rhythms of Africa

One example of a successful power2give program is Embrace Music Foundation's acclaimed Rhythms of Africa program.[10] A group of forty at-risk youth musical novices were selected to study the historical and cultural roots of African percussion instruments, learn to play in an ensemble, and then perform with internationally renowned musicians.

Developed by Willie "Reggae Ambassador" Stewart, former percussionist and co-director of the international group Third World, Rhythms of Africa/Music around the World describes the movement of ancient rhythms sprung from the souls of vibrant cultures and carried by hand and heart from Africa to the Caribbean, South America, and the New World. It is truly the rhythms of the diaspora, seasoned by time and cultivated and rooted by generations of pilgrims.

Through the intensive seven-week program, the students learned the roots of African music and studied singing, dancing, and drumming, using dozens of percussion instruments, all of which culminated in a public performance. Through this program, children grasped a vision of themselves as artists and performers admired by the audience for their achievements and were prepared to explore further opportunities in the arts.

Sculpting Lives

Local Fort Lauderdale ceramic artist Steven Sylvester is known for his uncommon use of clay in life-size women's dresses. Sylvester also created a program called Sculpting Lives to positively impact disadvantaged youth through the use of art and to build community awareness of the "aging out" foster care population.[11] The project occurs in several sessions where participants design, sculpt, and glaze ceramic art "homes" and, finally, participate in a written or oral reflective exercise that will help to wrap up their unique experiences. With a background in social work, Sylvester brings a unique perspective to the concept combining art, therapy, and introspection.

The hope is to not only have youth reflect on their lives but also to help them make valuable connections with community members who may later serve as mentors or help to shape a positive image and perception about various community agencies such as the fire department, police agencies, guardians ad litem, and so on.

Classroom conversations include building relationship skills and creating participants' own homes and families. A major component of this project is linking youth participants with community members and leaders, who become mentors. Some program partners have been Entertainment Benefits Group, Guardian Ad Litem, HANDY's (Helping Abused Neglected and Disadvantaged Youth) Next Gen Auxiliary Committee and HANDY's Alumni Associations, the Broward Sheriff's Office, the fire department, and HandsOn Broward. Online donors for the project were also given the opportunity to interact with the youth and attend the clay-building classes.

Rhythms of Africa and Sculpting Lives are just two examples of the ways the community was able to support the arts either financially or through participation and bring civic engagement and art together for a greater cause. The power of using the arts to address issues of public concern has had a big impact on our community.

ART IN THE WORKPLACE

Art in the Workplace, another program by Business for the Arts of Broward, is designed to forge lasting relationships between the arts community and local businesses. It provides arts awareness, involvement, and enrichment to employees at work. Through this program, an organization can bring art to the workplace by inviting an artist or musician to conduct a workshop for the employees or invite a local artist to display or perform his or her work for the employees to enjoy.

The program has positively impacted employees and businesses by bringing various disciplines of the arts directly into the workplace. Classes include a variety of offerings, such as ceramics, painting, printing, textiles, recycled art, book deconstructing, wine glass painting, origami, quilling, chocolate art, Japanese flower arranging, *gyotaku* (traditional Japanese fish prints), Hawaiian dance and music, song writing, and percussion. All are hands on, engaging, and nonthreatening approaches for staff to feel comfortable and successful in creating and participating in the experiences.

The Art in the Workplace program has been an innovative way to bring art to the business community and strengthen the bond between arts and the community. The primary focuses are art appreciation and education, stress relief, team building, and cooperation. Providing meaningful ways to support and foster new connections with local artists and business has been a positive outcome of the program, which has reached nearly a thousand employees since its inception in 2012. Often we see that when people engage in an arts activity, they begin to look at other arts opportunities perhaps for the first time, and a newfound appreciation is born.

ARTIST LIVE/WORK SPACES

Sailboat Bend Artists' Lofts

Sailboat Bend Artists' Lofts opened in February 2008, with thirty-seven professional visual and performing artists moving into the affordable live/work space. Artspace Projects, Inc., a Minneapolis-based not-for-profit real estate developer for the arts, contracted with Broward County for the development of these affordable apartments, which feature large, open floor plans that include gallery space for all types of art.[12] Its purpose is to give artists the opportunity to live and work in affordable one-, two- or three-bedroom residences, ranging from five hundred to more than one thousand square feet. This joint venture has created an environment where artists can live and work alongside each other in the heart of downtown Fort Lauderdale as part of a thriving cultural community. Each floor has a gallery in the center, and monthly art exhibitions feature artists from Sailboat Bend as well as other local artists, both emerging and professional.

While the Fort Lauderdale lofts are the first of their kind in Florida, Artspace Projects has created similar artist communities in Connecticut, Illinois, Minnesota, and Maryland.

The Florida project, which took almost ten years to plan, has become a model for the arts community, its patrons, and supporters. The Sailboat Bend Artists' Lofts launched with overwhelming results as artists vied to be accepted. Each artist must meet financial requirements for the minimum and maximum income allowed and be juried in based on his or her artwork and résumé.

Combining a historical restoration, an arts project with new housing, and a new home for the historical commission in a historic neighborhood, the concept was a recipe for success. Today the facility is home to some of the best professional artists and has a consistently filled waiting list.

Studio 18 in the Pines

A similar project is Studio 18 in the Pines, which was modelled after the Sailboat Bend concept but as an artists' studio work space rather than a living space. A vacant building was renovated into an eleven-thousand-square-foot facility that houses both inside and outside fine artists' studios as well as gallery and classroom space. The rents are affordable for local emerging and professional artists, who have to be juried in to sign a year lease. Funded entirely by the City of Pembroke Pines and resident support in a general operating bond, the facility became an innovative example of the foresight and vision that a municipality can and should invest in.

Artspace Projects is interested in creating a second facility in the Fort Lauderdale area and is working with the county to investigate possible new locations. We now see other surrounding cities following the model and expanding artists' work spaces in other parts of the county, most recently in the cities of Pompano Beach and Lauderhill. Residents and the community are now able to interact directly with artists where they work, attend affordable arts classes, participate in free gallery openings, and have a sense of pride in their local arts communities. Everyone from an art novice to the experienced art patron can attend events in venues such as these and feel welcomed.

Inside Out

As part of their centennial celebration, Broward County has partnered with a Parisian street artist known as JR for his *Inside Out*, a global art project. The idea is to give communities all over the world a platform to express themselves through black-and-white photographs. JR created the original concept and installations with large-format street pastings of photographs. *Inside Out* gives everyone the opportunity to share their portrait and make a statement and captures a collective message through headshots of individuals, which are printed on posters, pasted on public spaces, and archived online. This global platform allows people to tell their untold stories and transform messages of personal identity into works of public art. Since 2007, installations have appeared on walls, sidewalks, streets, skyscrapers, and historic buildings around the globe. Each installation around the world is documented, archived, and exhibited online to tell stories of community groups, and more than 120,000 people from more than 108 countries have participated.[13]

Broward College is a higher education cornerstone in Broward County, Florida, which is embarking on a yearlong journey to celebrate one hundred years of history through the arts and culture of its residents and titled its *Inside Out* project *I Am the Voice of Innovative Education and Civic Engagement in the 21st Century. Broward 100—Celebrating the Art of Community*, will bring diverse groups together to tell their stories, share experiences, and make new connections using the arts as a universal form of communication.

CONCLUSION

Civic engagement can be a measure or a means of social change. In arts-based civic engagement, the creative process and resulting artwork/experience can provide a key focus, catalyst, or space for civic participation, either by community members becoming better informed or actively contributing. It's not a question of whether or not the arts are important and useful tools for engagement. It's a matter of sharing the vision, appreciation, and opportunity for the creative process to purposefully improve one's neighborhood, community, and nation.

From the very first time man started to create art with elegant lines and rich colors on cave walls to modern urban murals on city streets, we have been compelled to express ourselves through art. The media may have changed, but the message is the same: I am here; I observe what is around me; and I am influenced by it. Acknowledging that the arts are an essential part of life and the key to a thriving society, let us be inspired to become stronger advocates for public art and engagement.

NOTES

1. Broward County Cultural website, http://www.broward.org/arts.
2. Imagination Squared, http://imaginationsquared.com/.
3. UrbanPopSoul.com, http://www.urbanpopsoul.com/#!landscape/cyuu.
4. Proposal to Arts & Culture Advisory Board of Pembroke Pines. Title: The Community, Date: April 16, 2012.
5. Americans for the Arts, http://www.AmericansForTheArts.org.
6. Jarett S. Levan, President of BBX Capital (Personal email communication with Robyn Vegas on February 2, 2015).
7. Nanette Saylor, Director of Trash2Treasure (Personal email communication with Robyn Vegas on May 19, 2014).
8. Juliet Roulhac, Regional Manager of External Affairs, Florida Power & Light Company (Personal email communication with Robyn Vegas on May 21, 2014).
9. "Projects," power2give, http://www.power2give.org/broward.
10. Ibid.
11. Ibid.
12. "Sailboat Bend Artist Lofts/Historic West Side School," Artspace, http://www.artspace.org/our-places/sailboat-bend-artist-loftshistoric-west-side-school.
13. "Broward 100," Broward County website, http://www.broward.org/broward100.

6

The Intersection of Business and Public Art

How to Engage Businesses and Citizens in Public Art

Mary Allman-Koernig

INTRODUCTION

In its fourth year, *Art 2C on Havana* is a public/private partnership between the Havana Business Improvement District (BID) and the City of Aurora, Colorado's Art in Public Places Program (AIPP). Havana Street is the border line between the cities of Denver and Aurora, Colorado. Before the BID was formed, Havana Street was considered a place of dying retail and used car lots. Buckingham Square, a mall that opened in 1971 and then closed in 2007, became The Gardens on Havana in 2013. This streetscaped mall began the reinvention of retail business on Havana Street. One of the best ways to measure this reinvention is by looking at the retail vacancy rate. In 2010, at the beginning of the Havana Business Improvement District, the retail vacancy rate stood at 8.6 percent. By 2014, the vacancy rate had fallen to 2.3 percent. Since the BID's beginning, participating businesses have seen a significant increase in property valuations, and the City of Aurora has realized a double-digit growth in sales tax generated in the district. This growth is due, in part, to the City of Aurora's public art program. This chapter will investigate how involving businesses, in partnership with local government, can create an environment encouraging development, business growth, and civic engagement using public art.

HISTORY OF AURORA AND THE ART
IN PUBLIC PLACES PROGRAM

The City of Aurora, Colorado, was first incorporated as the town of Fletcher on April 30, 1891. Aurora has grown to 154 square miles and to a population of 347,953,[1] making Aurora the third-largest city in the state of Colorado and the fifty-fifth largest city in the United States. The diversity of Aurora's population is remarkable. In the Aurora Public Schools, 139 languages are spoken, a number rumored to be second only to New York City. According to the U.S. Census Bureau, 28 percent of Aurora's population identifies as Hispanic or Latino, 15 percent as black or African American, 4 percent as Asian, and 16 percent as some other race or two or more races.

The Art in Public Places program of Aurora began in 1993 with the passage of an ordinance requiring 1 percent of all above-ground capital investment to be set aside for public art. Once the ordinance passed, the Art in Public Places Commission was established, comprised of nine Aurora citizens appointed by the city council, one of who was required to be a professional visual artist. The first public art project was completed in 1997 at the Saddle Rock Golf Course. Titled *A Change in Rules*, the artwork is a tribute to the American Indian population who first occupied the land. From 1993 to 2000, the program experienced steady growth. By 2000, the first public art manager was hired. There are over 240 individual pieces of public art.

THE BEGINNING OF THE *ART 2C ON HAVANA* PROCESS

The idea of leasing sculptures for display in public areas has been growing by leaps and bounds across the United States. In Colorado alone, there are fifteen cities with programs designed to display sculpture along a variety of streetscapes. *Art on the Corner* (AOTC) in downtown Grand Junction is one of the oldest exhibitions. It is free to the public and includes more than one hundred sculptures in a variety of mediums and styles. The program has been recognized and mimicked in communities across the world. Another program in Colorado Springs, *Art on the Streets*, began in 1999. Since that time, more than two hundred works of art have been displayed throughout the downtown area of the city.

Looking at the success of these programs in other communities, Gayle Jetchick, executive director of the Havana BID, came to a meeting of the Art in Public Places Commission and expressed interest in a public/private partnership to create a similar program for the Havana BID. The Havana BID was formed in 2007 by a vote of its stakeholders to voluntarily agree to a 4.5 mill levy increase on commercial property collected by Arapahoe County. A mill represents one-thousandth of a dollar, based on the business's property valuation. This voluntary tax is collected by the county and then allocated to the BID. In 2013, this mill levy allocation came to a total of $377,992 and is estimated at $474,250 for the 2015 year. The district was formed by a vote of its stakeholders—that is, the business owners and property owners within the district, which stretches 4.3 miles along Havana Street from 6th Avenue to Dartmouth Avenue. The Havana BID corridor represents the westernmost boundary of Aurora, with neighboring city Denver abutting the western side of the street. The BID works to brand the district and encourage new investment. The BID sponsors special projects and events that attract customers and new business to the district.

These projects and events have included such initiatives as the creation and place-ment of "On Havana Street" district markers; the Havana Motor Mile project, pro-moting Havana Street as the place to buy a new or used car and have it serviced; and the Hidden Cash Event, which encouraged individuals and families to follow clues on Twitter leading them to a piece of public art where an envelope of Monopoly money was hidden that could then be traded in for real cash that afternoon. This event resulted in over three hundred new Twitter followers and dozens of selfies in front of various sculptures. The Seventh Annual Crusin' Havana Car Show featured five thousand classic cars and brought over twenty thousand people to the district.

In 2009, the city started a program called the All 4 Business Initiative in an effort to address concerns of business owners within the city regarding how city employees interacted with the business community. There were over three hundred participants in this process who collectively made over a thousand comments, criticisms, and suggestions about the City of Aurora's development process and customer service. This included how the city interacted with developers and business owners. The All 4 Business Committee worked with the Planning and Development Services of the city to redefine how site plans were delivered as well as worked with the Permit Of-fice to assist with contractors to more easily obtain building permits.

At a workshop conducted by the City of Aurora's Art in Public Places pro-gram that same year, citizens were asked where public art should be located. The workshop participants were notified through announcements made at town hall meetings held by members of the city council, as well as through direct contact via email. Attended by about fifty citizens, representatives from the Havana BID strongly expressed their desire to see a leased art program for the business corri-dor. In addition, the city agreed to fund concrete bases (which would serve as the foundations for sculptures), engineering fees, and costs associated with releasing a call to artists. The BID agreed to pay artist stipends, printing and marketing costs, as well as expenses for opening reception.

The first year proved challenging to convince business owners to lease a small por-tion of their property to the city for a dollar, signing a lease agreement, and provid-ing easements to access the art location for installation and de-installation. The city helped to identify a ten-square-foot area of private property as well as an easement allowing city vehicles to access the space for sculpture installation and de-installation. The location of the artwork pad is determined by several factors. The first is in con-sultation with the business owners or their representatives, determining where the artwork would be best placed for safety and aesthetic factors. Next, the city surveyor determines easements to the site, checks for utilities and other easement restrictions, and then creates a simple lease form. However, each succeeding year, more and more property owners came forward requesting to be included in the program. Beginning with just ten property owners, there are now thirteen leased spaces and one space that was given to the Art in Public Places program for a purchase made after the first year. This artwork, titled *Tween*, is a cast bronze figure of a young girl with pony tails holding a rabbit in her hands. It is permanently on display in the rose garden, a public area in the Gardens on Havana shopping streetscape mall. The Havana BID currently has a waiting list for businesses wanting to participate in the program. The Art in Public Places Commission has set a maximum number of sites at fifteen through 2019, at which time the program will be reassessed to determine if more sites should be included in the program.

Dancing Moon Velocity is yet another piece in the collection. It is a colorful and playful sculpture that relates childhood memories to the natural world. This bright and multicolored sculpture attracts the attention of visitors and passersby.

THE PROCESS OF COMMUNITY
AND BUSINESS ENGAGEMENT

As with all public art projects, the first stage is to submit a "call to artists" defining the parameters of the art, such as height and safety concerns. These concerns included what the site could accommodate, such as width and height; specified safety concerns, such as sharp edges; or what could be termed as "attractive nuisances," such as climbing ability. The call includes a brief description of the city of Aurora, of the BID, and time frames for installation and de-installation. Also spelled out for the artists is the stipend and cash prizes to be awarded. Once the submittals are in, a selection panel is convened to choose the sculptures for the yearlong exhibit. The selection panel is chosen through a process of asking the community who may be interested in serving. First, members of the Havana BID are asked to serve, and then business members who will feature a piece of art are asked to participate. Then community members who live in the vicinity are asked to participate by inviting them through town hall meetings and online requests. The names of those who wish to participate are presented to the executive director of the Havana BID to be vetted regarding community involvement and suitability to serve on the panel. The artwork is selected based on the interest of the business community, the artistic merit, and the ability of the art work to fit into the specified sites.

The next step is to assign the individual artworks to the participating businesses. This selection is based on what the business owners have expressed about their likes and dislikes as well as the sculpture's size and shape in relation to the site's engineering specifications for what the concrete pad can accommodate. On several occasions, the committee's selection was not what the business owner desired, so an additional three to four sculptures are included as alternates.

Engaging the community is where *Art 2C on Havana* comes alive. The community is asked to vote on a "People's Choice" award. People's Choice voting is promoted through website newsletters and press releases, and incentives are offered to tour the art and vote. Gift certificates, some donated by local businesses and others purchased by the BID, are used to encourage voting. Everyone is encouraged to participate, and we have found that a lot of interest is generated by the artists themselves, hoping to promote their work. In 2012, we used actual paper ballots at participating businesses. The next year the ballot was online, both on the city's website as well as on the district's website.

The Havana BID uses *Art 2C on Havana* for various promotions, such as newsletter advertisements and business promotions, involving all ages and backgrounds. In March of 2015, the BID hosted a special event using social media as a way of reaching the millennials in the community. Called the Hidden Cash Event, Monopoly money was hidden at locations featuring pieces of art from the *Art 2C on Havana* exhibition. Every hour beginning at 8 a.m., a clue was sent via Twitter leading participants to the hidden cash. Over three hundred Twitter followers participated in the event, and $500 was awarded at the end of the day at a local restaurant.

For other events, participating artists are asked to come and talk about how they create their individual sculptures. One such presentation that attracted a large audience came from a sculptor whose medium is bronze, during which he explained the "lost wax" technique used in making his sculptures. Another artist, who works with reclaimed metals and found objects, talked about how he creates his work. These types of events help to bring the public and the artists together. They are both educational and fun. The audiences enjoy interacting with the artists and learning about specific techniques used on pieces of art they may see regularly throughout the city.

The City of Aurora prints brochures that depict the art and their locations along the Havana Corridor. These brochures are distributed at the local businesses and at various meetings throughout the city and the metro area. The public and tourists can use the brochures to identify pieces they want to visit, and it has become a way to promote the Art in Public Places program.

The success of the *Art 2C on Havana* exhibition lies with the public/private partnership developed between the City of Aurora and the Business Improvement District. A program such as this is stronger with the support of the city and the BID, as well as the support driven by the participating business owners. *Art 2C on Havana* is consistently cited as one of the most popular and significant projects done by the BID. The 2014 annual report cites that their expenditure of $25,000 leveraged bringing over $161,000 worth of art to the district. The BID is on board to grow the program to fifteen locations and has a waiting list of businesses anxious to participate.

PUBLIC ART AND ECONOMIC DEVELOPMENT

Over and over, communities are learning how public art can be an economic driver by creating unique and sometimes whimsical streetscapes. Although anecdotal at this stage, an argument can be made that *Art 2C on Havana* has participated in the phenomenal economic growth of the Havana corridor. During the last four years, the Havana Corridor has experienced a 21 percent increase in assessed valuation (Arapahoe County). During that same four years, sales tax revenue generated by the Havana Corridor for the City of Aurora has seen a 17 percent increase. In the last two years, 110 net new businesses have opened, creating 590 jobs. Of course, public art is not the only reason for this dramatic increase, but it can be argued that the desirability to do business along the corridor has been enhanced by public art.

CONCLUSION

The effect of public art on economic growth and creating great places to live and work is evident from this small example. As more communities invest in public art, whether through leased programs or with permanent installations, the ability for communities to engage their constituents, businesses, and customers will prove to be a viable way to secure a solid economic future. Cities must be willing to engage the public in nontraditional ways. Using Twitter to engage millennials with Monopoly money is one example. In addition, the business community must be engaged and recognized as an important part of the public. Bringing the public, business community, and local government together into a partnership has created a solid Art in Public Places program.

NOTE

1. United States Census Bureau, http://quickfacts.census.gov/qfd/states/08/0804000.html

7

Civic Engagement as Part of Evaluating and Adopting Adaptive Public Art Policies

Sherri Brueggemann

INTRODUCTION

Community engagement, or lack thereof, can have significant impacts on public art policy. How public art is funded, selected, managed, and, in some cases, removed are regularly influenced by the level of community involvement. While community engagement may seem to imply that only the external public is directly involved, internal participants also count as part of the public in public art. The City of Albuquerque Public Art Program's thirty-six-year history serves as a case study for how public art policy adapts over time to internal and external influences. This chapter will explore how internal influences (elected or administrative officials, boards or commissions and staff) and external influences (local citizen participants and national trends) affect the adaptability of public art policy. Four specific public art policies will be reviewed to illustrate how policy shifts over time to address public art funding and intent, community representation in the art procurement process, and intellectual property concerns. Leadership of other established and emerging public art programs can learn from the policy shifts experienced by the Albuquerque program to better anticipate their own policy adaptability.

The City of Albuquerque adopted its 1 Percent for Art Ordinance on November 22, 1978. Since then, nearly all of the enabling, guiding, and internal policies and documents have been modified in some form, from complete rewrites to minor edits. Each time, engaged citizens at various levels were involved in the policy evolution process. The resulting policies have become more adaptable, and the program itself has become more responsive to the public, especially by procuring works of art that have a strong sense of place and help build community.

In order to evaluate the long-term adaptability of the public art–related policies, I created a causal model using a seven point *adaptive policy analysis theory*, which examines the policy intent, structure, and adaptive capacity. After an in-depth historical context and content review of the changes to the public art policy, the findings show that public art program policy evolution that includes civic engagement at various levels over time supports program longevity.

Government-enabled public art programs are abundant in the United States,[1] having proliferated at a rapid pace since the first programs were established in the mid-twentieth century. Government-funded public art programs tend to have fairly significant budgets, equaling between 0.5 percent and 2 percent of entire municipal and/or state capital outlay budgets, often resulting in millions of public dollars designated for art acquisition. However, public art programs are still at risk of being defunded, eliminated, or unable to be created when an economic crisis hits government budgets. Public art program administrators and arts advocates must continually prove the value of their programs to those elected officials and citizens who believe that the funds should be used for more critical benefits and services.

Public art program evaluation has yet to be significantly impacted by a single standardized model that is widely embraced by professional public art administrators. According to the sources reviewed,[2] establishment of a single unified model is highly unlikely within the field. Approaches to public art evaluation waver between evaluating the artworks in a collection, the process by which they were commissioned or acquired, and the public art program itself and its objectives. Evaluating a public art program purely from a policy perspective over the course of a mature public art program's lifespan is a new approach. Of the more than six hundred public art programs throughout the United States, approximately half are established by ordinance and follow somewhat similar processes for art procurement and collection management. Evaluating the adaptability of public art policy (e.g., ordinances, procurement guidelines, and contractual management) may be the first step in considering the role of the public in affecting best practices in public art policy.

ADAPTIVE POLICY THEORY

The study of adaptive policy is a relatively new area of policy analysis. The term "adaptive policy" emerged in the early 1990s in reference to natural resource and environmental management policy development in the United States. The primary approach to adaptive policy development and analysis is based on an understanding that much governmental work is being done with a sense of rapid and dramatic change in the world: climatic, economic, political, and social. Such rapid changes, sometimes anticipated and sometimes not, are causal influences that must be grappled with in real time while trying to look toward the future. While public art is not as critical as lowered worldwide food production due to climate change or the melting of polar icecaps, the economic effects of public art program elimination or the inability to gain support for initiating a new program could be significant at the local level. The adaptive capacity of policy deals as much with anticipated and unanticipated conditions that affect a program and its implementation as it does with internal and external influences.

The primary type of adaptive policy is the "no-regrets policy," wherein the core policy continues to perform under a wide range of conditions without needing modification.[3] The policy is designed from the beginning to hold up against most, if not all, anticipated conditions of implementation. In addition to considering internal, external, anticipated, and unanticipated factors, seven fundamental principles apply to policies with strong adaptive capacity. Those principles are (1) integrating a forward-looking analysis of the policy environment by respecting the past, (2) including multistakeholder deliberation, (3) providing for automatic policy adjustment, (4) enabling self-organization, (5) decentralizing decision making, (6) promoting variation within policies, and (7) utilizing formal policy review and continuous learning. Adaptive policy theory emphasizes an understanding of the policy environment, which is highly dynamic, unpredictable and uncertain itself. An unprepared policy in such a setting has a good chance of not achieving its objective, or worse, having unintended negative consequences. Civic engagement in policy evaluation and modification can help assure that public art policies and programs have longevity and continue to build community.

PUBLIC ART POLICY TYPES

Municipal percent-for-art programs typically operate based on four types of polices: (1) distributive policy, enabled legislatively, which defines the funding mechanism; (2) governance policy, which defines the decision-making process; (3) institutional policy, also known as administrative rulemaking; and (4) regulatory policy, which defines the day-to-day operations. Distributive policy is defined as policy that seeks to "distribute a good or benefit to some portion of the population" in a cooperative and noncompetitive manner, that through a "universalistic" view provides "something for everyone."[4] Distributive policy, established through legislative action, allocates money from one source to another. Local enabling legislation, in most cases an ordinance, establishes a public art program and defines the amount of funds to be allocated toward art. Therefore, legislation enacted by municipal political actors, usually at the request of citizens, that creates an ordinance to establish a public art program and defines the source and use of funds for art acquisition is the distributive policy.

Governance policy has two functions in the governmental realm: to connect the public with government administration (primarily through appointed boards and commissions) and to provide for the manageable and accountable authority of such appointed bodies.[5] Governance policy is born out of social contract theory. Through a social contract model, a public organization that engages in public enterprise has the obligation to act on behalf of the general public, who are the owners of such enterprises. Governance policy manifests in public art programs through the public art advisory board. Taken directly from the distributive policy, the roles and duties of the appointed advisory board typically include establishing a set of bylaws and/ or codes of conduct for themselves and the program, respectively. The bylaws for a public advisory board for a public art program are intended to govern the board itself and account for its sense of self-organizing for the purpose of managing the public's interest in acquiring art.

Institutional policy and/or administrative rule making in public art programs affect a broad spectrum of issues, ranging from human resources management policy, which affects the makeup and functioning of program staff, to procurement methods, or to artists' payment procedures for services rendered. Institutional policy and administrative rule making are "structured by procedures that are designed to ensure agency decisions are informed by the views of affected interests."[6] Institutional policy has the goal of creating responsive, procedural, and political accountability as an extension of the legislative process. The Albuquerque Public Art Program guidelines, the broadest set of institutional policies, govern the process by which artworks are procured, including defining the civic engagement process. This type of policy directly connects the public to the government and provides for stakeholder input throughout the process of procuring art.

Regulatory policy that affects public art can also take on a variety of issues, both internal and external to the program and its parental department. Requiring engineering design review for artwork structure and safety as well as insurance requirements for the artists are two examples of municipal regulatory policies enacted by other departments or agencies that affect public art. The intellectual property clause of the public artwork contract, in which ownership and control of copyright and moral rights are defined, is an example of an internal policy that is regulatory.

INTELLECTUAL PROPERTY POLICY

Intellectual property is an area of public art policy frequently discussed among practitioners, especially artists, as an indicator of a public art program's "philosophy." There is a special section of the United States copyright law dealing specifically with visual art in the public realm, the Visual Artists Rights Act of 1990 (VARA). This regulatory policy area is highly specialized. Intellectual property in the field of public art includes both the economic rights of reproduction and distribution as well as the artists' rights of attribution and nondestruction or alteration. Moral rights are concerned with actions toward the art, such as alterations, removal, and destruction of works of art that are prejudicial to the artist's reputation. While economic rights can be transferred, licensed, or sold, moral rights are not transferable and belong only to the artist who created the artwork. In the United States, both sets of rights were not always available to artists. The national public art controversy over Richard Serra's *Tilted Arc* in the 1980s[7] fostered the federal codification of moral rights that European artists enjoyed since the nineteenth century, also known as *droits moral*. The codification of those rights in the United States became a regulatory policy requiring any art commissioning body, public or private, to ensure the protection of artists' reputations by establishing procedures for removal, modification, relocation, or destruction of public art.

When looking at public art policy and adaptability with regard to internal and external influences, the effects of *Tilted Arc* and VARA are undeniable and provide a solid grounding for marking time and national cultural shifts that affect public art policy nationwide. Intellectual property law is critical to public art program administration, and, therefore, the contractual clauses related to copyright and VARA in the case study were selected as the regulatory policy to be evaluated in the same manner as the distributive, governance, and institutional policies to determine overall policy adaptability.

UNDERTAKING THE POLICY EVALUATION

Throughout thirty-six years of procuring nearly 850 artworks, the Albuquerque Public Art Program has maintained a relatively complete set of all advisory board meeting minutes, all ordinance revisions with accompanying annotation and commentary, and digital and hard copy project files for each work of art, noting the community engagement and art selection (procurement) process, financial data, and executed contracts. The program has also aggressively collected "media files," including news stories, articles, and promotional collateral materials for each work of art. To make accessing the data for each project easy, the program has compiled a detailed collection database with forty-two fields per record on each work of art, ranging from artists' names and addresses to artwork categories, sizes, materials used, and costs. This comprehensive collection of official documentation, which has been consistently well organized and maintained throughout three and a half decades, was utilized extensively to research policy adaptations and nuances throughout the program's history.

While this extensive trove of program and project documentation is critical to understanding the internal influences, other sources have been consulted to establish a history of the broader cultural and public art policy environment to help identify external influences. Public art history articles, books, and internal nonpolicy program documents[8] provide the most useful sources to begin to piece together the actual causal factors of the policy changes in the case study data.[9]

DEVELOPING THE CAUSAL MODEL

With the internal and external context established, the case study policies are analyzed based on their responsiveness to internal and external conditions as well as anticipated and unanticipated factors. This step determines if the policy being revised is more likely to meet the seven adaptive policy principles, especially the civic engagement principles, than before the revision. For the causal model diagram (figure 7.1), the inputs are the different types of causal factors on the efficacy of policies. The outputs are policies that have been changed due to internal, external, anticipated, and unanticipated conditions and factors, or any combination thereof. The outcomes are the degree to which the changed policies became either more or less adaptive (i.e., expressive of the evolving community and based on the seven principles of adaptive policy). The outcome of changed policy can be immediate addressing citizens concern right away, short to midterm affecting decision making and process on the next project pursued, or long range, building trust in the community and stability for the program. Additionally, the type of outcome can vary depending on the causal factor with the most influence.

The causal diagram is structured by hierarchically categorizing the types of policies reviewed (distributive, governance, institutional, and regulatory), identifying the different types, of causal factors (internal, external, anticipated, and unanticipated), and finally considering the immediate, short- to midterm and long-range outcomes based on the seven principles of adaptability. The seven principles can have direct or indirect outcomes, with the ultimate outcome being that the core policy remains intact and functional, facilitating procurement of public art in a manner that includes civic engagement.

Figure 7.1 depicts a model that was developed by the author.[10] The model allows for the evaluation of adaptability of public art policy over the long term. The model is informed by existing cultural policy theory and emerging adaptive policy analysis frameworks through which the case study public art policy intent, structure, and adaptive capacity was examined for anticipated, unanticipated, internal, and external conditions.

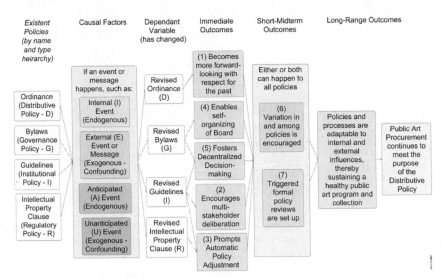

Figure 7.1.   Casual Logic Model[11]

FINDINGS AND ADAPTABILITY ANALYSIS

Distributive Policy—the Ordinance

The core of the Albuquerque Art in Municipal Places Ordinance has remained intact for thirty-six years. The original ordinance had forty-five clauses: six dedicated to the purpose, sixteen dedicated to the arts board and its powers and duties, seven dedicated to the funding mechanism, and eight dedicated to procuring art. The remaining eight clauses were perfunctory to ordinance writing, except for one that amended the overarching procurement code to exclude works of art from competitive bids and one that repealed the establishment of the previous arts advisory committees.

The ordinance was first revised in 1983 to increase the number of arts board members from seven to nine. This change was initiated by the mayor to correspond to the recent increase in the number of city council districts. Arts board members, at that time, were not appointed by their respective councilor, but the sitting mayor deemed the proportion of representatives on the arts board inadequate for the number of city council districts. The advisory board section of the ordinance was again changed four more times (in 2000, 2006, 2008, and 2012) to address responsiveness—or lack thereof—by both levels of municipal elected officials. In 2000, the board size was increased from nine to eleven as a result of an override of a mayoral veto to allow each city councilor to provide input regarding the appointment of arts board members from their districts and to allow the mayor to have two at-large members.[12]

In late 1991 and early 1992, however, the entire Art in Municipal Places Ordinance underwent a complete review and refinement as the result of a city council resolution directing the administration to "evaluate the current art in public places program."[13] Nary was a clause left untouched. The changes made throughout the ordinance were primarily to clean up old and outdated language and to clarify or expand the purpose and intent, but there were a few substantive changes that cannot go unnoticed in terms of adaptiveness to anticipated and unanticipated external conditions, those being tied to the massive controversy over a local artwork, and the NEA public art handbook, *Going Public*.[14]

In 1990, the selection and installation of a large outdoor sculpture embroiled the Albuquerque Public Art Program in a citywide controversy. The sculpture featured a real 1957 Chevy placed on an arch and covered in handmade turquoise and cobalt blue tiles.[15] A local radio personality who did not like the sculpture used his position on the air to generate awareness of the public artwork, the program, and the process used to select public art for the previous decade. The controversy erupted in the late summer of 1990 with countless letters to the editors, radio show call-ins, and local newspaper articles. By early spring 1991, the city council resolution calling for a complete program review was passed unanimously.

The resolution included eleven specific questions for the administration to address. The questions covered various issues, including benefits of the public art process being more participatory, diversity of the collection including more locations, artists' eligibility with regard to residency, and "defining the city's philosophy" about public art. The question of "philosophy" alluded to the long-term care of artworks.

As a result of the city council–mandated ordinance review, the policy was enhanced with clarifications and updates, but there was no substantial change to the original intent or purpose: the allocation of funds for art and an advisory board. Locations where art could be placed were expanded from only municipal property to include any publicly owned property, taking advantage of the opportunity to combine city 1 percent for art funds with other state or county 1 percent for art funds or funds from other governmental or institutional entities, such as the local university. Further, the mayor was no longer able to decide the budget to start a project or dictate timelines, this likely being a response to the entire capital improvements system becoming a much more complex process managed by professional project managers.

Other changes to the ordinance directly reflect the influence of the field guide to public art, *Going Public*. The field guide was a comprehensive review of best practices in the areas of public art administration and preservation. Other cities' programs and policies, such as Los Angeles, Miami, Phoenix, and Seattle, were introduced and discussed as models for public art programs that balanced public interests with those of artists. Case studies illustrating contract negotiations, public involvement strategies, and controversies were included. Half of the book is dedicated to the care and management policies of works of art after they are acquired by a public agency.

The most substantial change to the Albuquerque ordinance during this comprehensive review, most likely influenced by *Going Public*, regarded the amount of funds allocated for the "administrative costs of the program and to restore and conserve public works of art to protect public investment." The amount was increased from 10 percent to "up to 20% but not less than 15%."[16] The addition of a set allocation for conservation of the public artworks was precedent setting. Mandating a 20 percent administrative budget gave the program management the opportunity to provide better outreach, communications, and stewardship of the already ten-year-old public art collection.

While the ordinance of 1992 expanded the locations eligible for public art to include other publicly owned property, a community initiated change in late 2014 went another step further. A coalition of local artists, youth arts organizations, and Route 66 enthusiasts successfully initiated a request to allow public art on privately owned but publicly accessible walls and large-scale, vacated "orphan signs." Orphan signs, also known as blue sky signs, are abundant along Albuquerque's historical Route 66. Property owners often raze old roadside structures but leave the out-of-compliance large sign canisters in place because they are grandfathered into the sign ordinance. With no business left on site to promote, the orphan signs have become new frameworks for long-term temporary public art.

In December 2014, the city council approved a nationally unprecedented ordinance change to allow municipal percent for art funds to be used on private signs and walls, expanding the city's mural program and public/private partnership investments on Route 66. Once the engaged community and diverse constituents (unanticipated/external influence) presented the concept, the administration and city council worked interdepartmentally to resolve legal challenges. Just days after the city council vote to approve the ordinance change, the local daily newspaper ran an editorial in support of the amendment[17] encouraging the mayor to waste no time signing the legislation into law.

The changes to the ordinance reflect a variety of conditions that can necessitate adaptation. Many types of internal and external conditions create anticipated or unanticipated events, but the effect on the core distributive policy remains minimal. The refinement and adjustment, however, reinforces the adaptive capacity of the policy over the long term by meeting the first and sixth adaptability principles: (1) to be more forward looking with respect for the past and (6) to introduce a greater variation of policies.

Governance Policy—the Bylaws

The first set of bylaws and rules of procedure were developed in late 1979 and adopted in February of 1980. Early drafts show that they were adapted from boilerplate bylaws for other boards and commissions within the municipal government at the time. Since 1980, the bylaws have only been changed six times, with the last revisions being adopted in spring 2013. Formatting changes to the bylaws in the first revision of 1992 included "chang[ing] the order of some of the paragraphs to bring them into conformance with proper parliamentary procedures."[18] Substantive changes affect primarily the governance features of the bylaws, enabling better organizational structure of the board itself. During the ten-year period between the initial bylaws and the first revision, the city hired two full-time program staff members who carried out many of the administrative duties previously performed by the arts board secretary and others. Therefore, certain board officer positions were eliminated. Board attendance appears to have been a significant issue, as several revisions specifically to encourage or mandate board meeting attendance were evident. These various technical revisions are categorized as internal/anticipated factors that affected the bylaws.

One addition of note that was anticipated due to an external situation was the "Resignations" section, wherein board members would henceforth be required to submit written letters of resignation to the mayor and copied to the chairperson. Many years earlier, a board member left the board without formal notification. Being an artist, the former member promptly applied for a public art project that was being developed while he was previously serving on the board. Not only did the former board member apply, but his art proposal was selected for the commission. The following month, a disgruntled, unselected, artist applicant wrote a harsh letter to the arts board and presented it in person, calling out the conflict of interest. The artist was well underway with the project and was allowed to finish the commission, even though several board members recognized the conflict of interest. Matters of conflicts of interest while serving on the arts board were included in the original bylaws at the time, but the issue of formal and documented resignations was not codified until almost ten years later.

Until 2013, an update to the bylaws had not been completed since 2001. A dedicated clause addressing the procedure for amending the bylaws stated that it must be done at a meeting of the board and a two-thirds majority must vote in favor, but there had been no reference to when a review or revision should be undertaken. In 2013, the bylaws were again reviewed and modified as a result of the policy adaptability analysis. Issues regarding the power of the chairperson over committee assignments; codes of conduct for board members toward staff, the public, and other board and committee members; and communications with elected officials were updated. A mandatory two-year review process that was also established during this revision, addressing the seventh adaptive policy principle, triggered formal review.

Adaptive policy theory suggests that a balance is required between allowing for informal self-organizing and governance in decentralized decision making. Appointed boards and commissions form their own process of social interaction around policymaking issues, which enables the group to explore and implement innovative solutions. While the flexibility of some self-organizing allows the advisory board to tackle challenges together, there also needs to be accountability to the public as the local stakeholders most affected by their decisions, especially when lower-level policymaking authority is delegated by ordinance to the board, and in some cases, through committees. Therefore, a set of bylaws for a public art advisory board that establishes an accountable and transparent linkage between different levels of government through good self-governance and public participation allows the board to be cohesive and able to respond to unexpected circumstances. Encouraging self-organizing is the fourth adaptive policy principle.

Institutional Policy—the Guidelines

By far, the case study public art policy that changed the most radically is the *City of Albuquerque Public Art Guidelines*. While there have only been four revisions after the original set in 1979, the content and format have undergone extensive changes. The original guidelines had only three sections: "Artist Selection," "Jury Selection and Responsibilities," and "Selection Process Review." The most current version has nine specific sections, with two new sections being developed to address the public art on private property ordinance changes.

As with the bylaws, the city council–mandated ordinance review of 1991 prompted the first revision of the guidelines. The guidelines were completely rewritten and only brief references to the original clauses remained. A set of definitions explaining public art policy–related terms, and a set of program goals were added. The most significant change was the process by which artists were selected for projects, which included a broadened community stakeholder role. The inclusion of more citizens in the art selection process was a direct result of the *Cruising San Mateo* controversy, wherein a committee of the arts board had been the sole jury members.

In the first guidelines, a committee of the arts board reviewed an artists' slide registry searching for viable candidates to be invited to submit an idea for a public art site. In the second version, a detailed description of the development of a prospectus and the role of the committee replaced the slide registry model, the latter becoming little more than a mailing list. This meant that the initial decision to participate in a new public art project had been shifted away from the small jury onto the artists. Additionally, the specific roles between the arts board and the committee, which was expanded to include citizen and user agency stakeholders, staff, and the artists were reflected throughout the entire new document.

The third version of the guidelines included the addition of two new goals, the minor modification of four sections including changing the name of the department under which the program resided, and clarification of the term "publicly owned" property, which allowed for municipal funds to be used on any type of government-owned property: city, county, state, or other. Stricter limits were placed on artist eligibility if the artist was already under contract for a public art project with the program. Cultural diversity and sensitivity were introduced as a goal, as were the protection and preservation of "all public art in Albuquerque which is not privately owned or cared for."[19] This last addition appears to have a direct correlation to the administrative funding clause change from 10 percent to no more than 20 percent and no less than 15 percent of the total amount for art was made available for the administrative costs of the program. The fourth revision of the guidelines took place in 2001. With numerous additions to the definitions section and clarifications throughout, the major changes in this version pertained to the art selection process. An entirely new section, with three clauses dealing with public art collection management, conservation, and deaccession of artworks, was also added.

As previously discussed, the adoption of the Visual Artists Rights Act of 1990 (VARA) had a profound affect on public art programs. The intent was to assure that visual works of art and the reputations of artists resulting from those works would be protected as long as feasibly possible. Nevertheless, the aging sculptures in public collections around the country were taxing sparse public art program resources. Removal of the art was often the only logical solution; hence, artwork deaccession policies and procedures were necessary for compliance with VARA. VARA allows for removal of art with proper notification to the artist and offers options ranging from repossession of the work by the artist to complete destruction so that no artwork element can exist in an altered, unapproved context.

Another new clause added to the 2001 guidelines was a previously developed stand-alone statement referred to as the "Appropriate Public Art Statement."[20] The statement, which is to be consulted by the arts board, committees, and staff, was drafted by the program manager in the late 1990s in response to a formal citizen complaint about a proposed temporary work of art (a burned American flag) for display in a city-owned gallery setting. The statement was adapted from the final version of the federal policy legislated by Congress in 1989, at the height of the culture war controversies.[21] The stand-alone statement was integrated into the "Artwork Criteria" section, thereby formalizing it as program policy.

The fifth and most current version of the guidelines was modified in 2011. Clarification of the roles and responsibilities of board, staff, and committee members, along with the inclusion of an entirely new decommission policy, made up the bulk of the revisions. Another entirely new section was the establishment of a new standing arts board committee and their responsibility to review "unsolicited proposals" for artwork.[22]

Regulatory Policy—Intellectual Property Clause

The case study data on intellectual property are abundant. With over seven hundred contracts available for review, the analysis of individual copyright and artwork modification or destruction clauses initially appears overwhelming. In analyzing the public art database, however, the majority of the projects (approximately three-quarters) were commissioned after the enactment of VARA in June 1990, rendering the majority of the intellectual property contractual clauses identical. In order to assess the adaptability of the intellectual property policy, a small sample of twenty of the over seventy contracts was used. The public art project contracts sampled were intentionally and carefully selected based on both the program history and historical evolution of artists' moral rights. Because New Mexico was one of a handful of states that adopted moral rights laws prior to the federal VARA,[23] evaluation of the policies was staggered in approximately three to five year intervals, with specific art projects in certain years selected. Among the hand-selected public art contracts were those with unique materials, locations, subject matter, artists with a high profile/stature in the field, and/or controversial art projects.

The intellectual property policy for public art is relatively straight forward, as copyright is a federal law and local governments must abide by the highest level of law. However, while sweeping copyright reform took place just two years before the case study ordinance was enacted, the moral rights went unaddressed for several additional years until states began to adopt such policies.[24] Copyrights can be transferred, assigned, or sold along with, or separate from, the final work of art. Moral rights are not transferable and are tied exclusively to the artwork. Because an artist "injects some of his or her spirit into the art . . . the artist's personality, as well as the integrity of the work, should be protected and preserved."[25] The disposition of an artwork directly affects the moral rights of the artist.

The earliest contract clauses for public art in the case study program are simple paragraphs that define the design materials and finished artwork as "instruments of service" in which the artist will retain all of the associated copyrights. Models, sketches, and drawings remain the tangible and intellectual property of the artist. The economic rights of reproduction of the artwork also remain with the artist except for the limited rights by the commissioning body to use photographic images of the artwork *as installed* for promotional and educational purposes. In early public art commission contracts, credit to the artist is about as close as the clause comes to granting moral rights. Within just a couple of years, the nondestruction/no alteration clause was introduced alongside the copyright clause. Between the late 1970s and mid 1980s, numerous accounts of sculptures and murals being relocated, altered, or destroyed throughout the country were making their way through the national media and arts publications. Articles were being written about the states adopting nondestruction or alterations laws partly in response to high-powered art collectors and museums doing what they wished with artworks they had acquired.[26] This external condition clearly began to affect the case study policy as early as 1983.

In 2000, an unanticipated copyright ownership and infringement struggle between members of a contracted public art project team (the artist and the fabricator) resulted in a mandatory joint copyright ownership for commissioned works of art between the artist and the city. The joint copyright ownership clause tightened up issues regarding subsequent use, reproduction of the artwork, and all related "instruments of service" so that any form of reproduction must be approved in writing by the city, especially for commercial purposes. The joint ownership also allows the city to use municipal resources (i.e., its own attorneys) to fight infringement because the municipality has direct ownership, a scenario that would not be allowed under the State of New Mexico's constitutional antidonation clause, wherein public resources cannot be used for private benefit.

CONCLUSION

Adaptive policy analysis is an emerging theoretical framework. The framework is based on policy adaptability to internal and external conditions coupled with anticipated and unanticipated causal factors. Applying this framework to the Albuquerque Public Art Program policies demonstrates how the seven principles of adaptive capacity become operable over the course of time, strengthening the core policies.

For the Albuquerque Public Art Program, the distributive policy enabled legislatively, the ordinance, is the "no-regrets policy" performing under various conditions with no wholesale changes. Since 1978, the ordinance has been modified only six times. One might say that there are no regrets about having a percent-for-art ordinance, even though there might be regrets about how the advisory board was appointed or how little funds were allocated for art conservation. The core of the distributive policy, the allocation of funds to procure art, and the existence of an advisory board to make recommendations on subsequent policy and art have been intact for thirty-six years. This demonstrates "policy robustness" per the adaptive policy model.

The comprehensive changes to the ordinance in 1991 and 1992 demonstrated the adaptability of the original policy in the face of a dynamic municipal policy environment and a changing political and evolving art world. On one hand, the core distributive intent was not modified. On the other hand, the multiple amendments rewording the arts board appointment process in the ordinance over a period of thirty-six years demonstrate the adaptability of the core policy to be more politically responsive and accountable over the long term. The fact that no other aspect of the core policy had been changed when "opened up" by the legislative body speaks to the validity and robustness of the core policy. While the 1991 city council mandated evaluation questions opened the door to many opportunities for the administration to niggle with the art selection and project management processes of the ordinance, the clarification revisions correctly left those details to be addressed in the lesser governance and institutional policies, the bylaws and guidelines.

The case study governance policies, bylaws, have been adjusted relative to minor internal/unanticipated factors. The most significant revision was the restructuring of the bylaws to reflect the revised ordinance. The board leadership structure, how committees are assigned, and the "Resignation" section are content changes most influenced by internal/anticipated factors. The most recently added board code of conduct is one of the more substantial changes to the bylaws as a direct result of participant engagement at all levels.

Guidelines for reviewing solicited and unsolicited art proposals; determining appropriateness of art in public spaces; and selecting, conserving, removing, or destroying public art are important policies for the proper functioning of a government public art program. Guidelines adjustments observed in the case study demonstrate that every combination of internal/external and anticipated/unanticipated conditions can cause a policy adjustment. Significant external conditions can substantially affect public art policy at the institutional level, such as local and national public art controversies, changes in national best practices, advancements in the field as a whole, and both technological development in and the failure of art materials. These types of conditions affect all seven principles of adaptive policy but are most informed by the role of civic engagement in the policy review and development process.

While embedded lesser policies within the guidelines are triggers for review throughout the art selection and management processes (i.e., the unsolicited proposals, appropriate art, and decommission policies), the entire set of guidelines do not contain a formal policy review clause. Informally, when the ordinance changes or the Albuquerque Public Art Program moves to a different department, a guideline review would likely take place. Interestingly, this lack of formal triggered review is one area in which the regulatory policy of intellectual property does not suffer.

Every contract executed by municipal government receives one, if not two, formal reviews by legal counsel. The intellectual property clause in the earliest public art contracts were simple and only addressed copyrights. As the moral rights debate ensued throughout the country and states like New Mexico adopted their own laws, the higher state policy had to be implemented at the municipal level. The eventual adoption of moral rights at the federal level trumped the state policy, leaving the municipality with very standardized intellectual property contract clauses for almost twenty years.

The change in external conditions around artists' moral rights had clear, definable, and immediate effects on the municipal intellectual property policy. New artworks were guaranteed to be free from modification or relocation, without following proper procedure. But, as older artworks began to deteriorate and experimental materials began to fail, public art program and legal staff utilized the waiver system as policy options for dealing with the anticipated long-term effects of deterioration in artwork materials. This is a textbook example of automatic policy review contributing to policy adaptive capacity principles of variation in policy and triggered formal reviews.

Evaluating the adaptive capacity of key Albuquerque Public Art Program policies proved to be an informative and defendable approach for public art program policy analysis. There were challenges to the data-coding process (e.g., determining a defining line between "internal" and "external" in municipal government or determining "who" anticipated or may not have anticipated changes in internal and external conditions). Municipal government involves many actors, and when conducting municipal business such as procuring public art, those boundaries can become quite blurred. Understanding the nuances of civic engagement provides the opportunity to evaluate the role of citizen and community input as part of the policymaking process.

NOTES

1. Americans for the Arts reports that there are approximately six hundred public art programs in the United States. http://www.americansforthearts.org/

2. Lambert 2006; Annabel Jackson Associates 2007; and Becker 2011.

3. Swanson and Bhadwal 2009.

4. Calavera 2008.

5. Carver 2001.

6. West 2004.

7. *Tilted Arc* by Richard Serra was a 120-foot-long, site-specific steel sculpture in the shape of a tilting wall, originally installed in 1981 on the Jacob Javits Federal Building Plaza in New York City. It was removed without the artist's consent, resulting in a lawsuit testing contractual obligations and censorship of artistic freedom under the First Amendment (Jordan and American Council for the Arts, 1987).

8. Selwood 1995; Wetenhall 2004; Zembylas 2004; Doss 2006; Tepper 2011.

9. One of the most seminal publications on public art policy, *Going Public: A Field Guide to Developments in Art in Public Places* (Cruikshank, Korza, and Andrews 1988) appears to have had a substantial impact on the program policies. Written in 1988 and published by the Arts Extension Service in collaboration with the Visual Arts Program of the National Endowment for the Arts, the field guide provided a detailed historical overview of the field up to its time and contains numerous program reviews and case studies of its own. This book, edited by Pam Korza, was the result of the National Public Art Policy Project. The entire book is dedicated to policy development from writing funding policies (ordinances) to long-term care

and maintenance of works of art once commissioned. Embedded are actual contracts, articles, essay reprints, and cataloguing and conservation forms. The introduction to *Going Public* lays out several philosophical ideals as a foundational reference for the rest of the book. These ideals proved most applicable in the review of influences on the case study public art policies.

10. Brueggemann 2013.

11. The terms "endogenous" and "exogenous-confounding" are used on the diagram in relation to the Swanson and Bhadwal (2009) adaptive policy theory.

12. The 2006, 2008, and 2012 ordinance modifications were also limited to the arts board appointment section of the ordinance to (1) "clarify the appointment process and allow for re-appointments" (O-2006-043, ROA 2006) in a clearer, less convoluted manner; (2) require a response from the mayor within thirty days to make an appointment (O-2008-008, ROA 2008); and (3) to require a councilor to respond within sixty days to make an appointment (O-2012-014, ROA 2012).

13. R-377, Ninth City Council 1991.

14. Cruikshank, Korza, and Andrews 1988.

15. The sculpture is titled *Cruising San Mateo I* by Barbara Grygutis, 1991.

16. O-24, ROA, 1992.

17. "Plan for Signs a Work of Art," *Albuquerque Journal*, December 5, 2014.

18. Albuquerque Arts Board 1992, 2.

19. Guidelines 1992.

20. Art suitable for public display may not include offensive subject matter such as the apparent representation of violence, inappropriate nudity, denigration of individuals or cultures, or desecration of significant cultural symbols. If the proposed artwork includes religious subject matter, the artwork must be able to be displayed in such a manner that the work is not revered and is solely for the purpose of exhibiting cultural or historical traditions (Guidelines 2012).

21. In response to the NEA funding photographs by artists Andres Serrano and Robert Mapplethorpe, Senator Jesse Helms had proposed language tied to the appropriations bill for that fiscal year's NEA funding. A modified version of Senator Helms's language regarding art appropriate for public funding was "eventually legislated into existence in October 1989" (McGuigan 2002) and provided the foundational language for the Albuquerque Appropriate Public Art policy: "Proposals for Works of Art that include subject matter such as the apparent representation of violence, inappropriate nudity, denigration of individuals or cultures, or desecration of significant cultural symbols, will be reviewed for their appropriateness for public display" (Guidelines 2001).

22. During the difficult economic climate of the last decade, the program received an unprecedented amount of proposals from artists to buy existing works, as large and higher-priced art was not moving in the retail art market. In order to address the deluge of requests from artists to review and consider purchasing existing art, a joint board/staff process was created to assure that such acquisitions met the intent of the program's goals and collection needs.

23. New Mexico's Act Relating to Fine Art in Public Buildings 1987.

24. *Going Public* (Cruikshank, Korza, and Andrews 1988) provides a snapshot of the pre-VARA years and the efforts leading up to the sweeping federal policy. Just three years before the Visual Artists Rights Act was passed, three states (California, New York, and Massachusetts) had adopted moral rights laws protecting artists and their works of art from intentional destruction or, in some cases, nonmalicious alteration of works of art (Failing 2002). Senator Edward Kennedy of Massachusetts had introduced VARA, presumably based on his own

state's policy, the same year *Going Public* was published. New Mexico adopted similar legislation in 1987. Therefore, the casual factor of the adoption of VARA emerged as an external/anticipated factor affecting intellectual property policy in the case study.

25. Lerner and Bresler 2006.
26. Cruikshank, Korza, and Andrews 1988.

REFERENCES

Annabel Jackson Associates. 2007. *Evaluation of Public Art: A Literature Review and Proposed Methodology.* Bath, UK: Annabel Jackson Associates. http://www.artscouncil.org.uk/media/uploads/yorkshireimages/2007AJAEvaluationofPublicArtLiteratureReviewPublicVersion.pdf.

Albuquerque Arts Board. 1992. *Minutes, January 21.*

Becker, J. 2004. "Public Art: An Essential Component of Creating Communities." *Monograph* (March).

———. 2011. "The Gospel of Public Art." *Public Art Review* 22 (2): 11.

Brueggemann, S. 2013. *An Informed Grounded Theory Approach to Public Art Policy Evaluation: Causal Factors for Adaptive Capacity Analysis,* Master's Professional Paper, University of New Mexico, School of Public Administration. http://www.cabq.gov/culturalservices/public-art/documents/SBrueggemannProPaperSpring2013.pdf.

Calavera, M. 2008. "The Role of Distributive Policy in Federal Government." Yahoo! Voices. http://voices.yahoo.com/the-role-distributive-policy-federal-government-2313570.html.

Carver, J. 2001. "A Theory of Governing the Public's Business: Redesigning the Jobs of Boards, Councils, and Commissions." *Public Management Review* 3 (1): 53–72.

City of Albuquerque Ordinances. 1978–2012.

Cruikshank, J. L., P. Korza, and Andrews, R. 1988. *Going Public: A Field Guide to Developments in Art in Public.* Edited by Pam Korza. Amherst, MA: Arts Extension Service, University of Massachusetts.

Doss, E. 2006. "Public Art Controversy: Cultural Expression and Civic Debate." *Monograph.*

Failing, P. 2002. *Artists Moral Rights in the United States before VARA.* Paper presented at the Committee on Intellectual Property of the College Art Association. http://www.studiolo.org/CIP/VARA/Failing/Failing.htm.

Fine Art in Public Buildings Section 13-4B-3—Fine Art; Alteration or Destruction Prohibited; Injunctive relief; Damages; Exceptions. New Mexico Statutes. 1995.

Jordan, S., and American Council for the Arts. 1987. *Public Art, Public Controversy: The Titled Arc on Trial.* Washington, DC: American Council for the Arts.

Lambert Ruley, S. 2006. *Public Art and Evaluation.* Baltimore: Goucher College.

Lerner, R. E., and J. Bresler. 2006. *PLI: Treatises—All about Rights for Visual Artists.* Volume 1 (p. 275). http://www.pli.edu/Content/Treatise/All_About_Rights_for_Visual_Artists/_/N-4lZ1z13i5t?ID=22354.

McGuigan, J. 2002. *Culture and the Public Sphere.* New York. Taylor & Francis.

Selwood, S. 1995. *The Benefits of Public Art: The Polemics of Permanent Art in Public Places.* London: Policy Studies Institute.

Swanson, D., and S. Bhadwal. 2009. *Creating Adaptive Policies: A Guide for Policy-making in an Uncertain World.* Ottawa: Sage, IDRC.

Tepper, S. J. 2011. *Not Here, Not Now, Not That! Protest over Art and Culture in America.* Chicago: University of Chicago Press.

West, W. F. 2004. "Formal Procedures, Informal Processes, Accountability, and Responsiveness in Bureaucratic Policy Making: An Institutional Policy Analysis." *Public Administration Review* (1): 66.

Wetenhall, J. 1993. "A Brief History of Percent-for-Art in America." *Public Art Review* 93 (9): 4.

Zembylas, T. 2004. "Art and Public Conflict: Notes on the Social Negotiation of the Concept of Art." Journal of Arts Management Law and Society 34 (2): 119–32.

8

A Community of
Narrators and Translators

Dee Hibbert-Jones

INTRODUCTION

This chapter describes creative art projects involving students, community members, artists, specialists, and others beyond fields of art. These collaborative projects were developed by artist fellows and affiliates of the Social Practice Arts Research Center (SPARC) at the University of California at Santa Cruz (UCSC), which I founded and now codirect at the UCSC with my colleagues, Associate Professor Elliot Anderson, Professor E. G. Crichton, and SPARC coordinator Kyle McKinley.

SPARC fosters knowledge exchange and project building between artists, scientists, the public, and others with a vision toward active social and environmental change. Bringing together diverse communities, SPARC supports the creation of artwork that addresses critical social, civic, and environmental issues in the public sphere. The role and value of public art within a community is a critical question for a research center housed in an academic institution that resides in a small city. The city of Santa Cruz is known for its surf, agricultural produce, political activism, as well as proximity to Silicon Valley, and hence high property prices. The role of public art in this community is fundamental. The community welcomes creative arts engagement, and this is a pivotal moment for engagement and dialogue to emerge through public art projects. Many of the issues facing the city can be seen as a microcosm of the larger issues that face the national population, a divided city racially and economically, with land and environmental issues at the fore and the issue of housing as a new class of Silicon Valley wealth hits the city. Public art can engage and unify this diverse and vibrant community.

ART AS PEDAGOGY, ART AS RESEARCH

Housing a creative arts practice within a university offers a unique set of resources and also questions. Despite limited monetary resources, the university is still rich in other resources. The university brings intellectual access; experts in other fields; physical sites for art making; venues for congregation; and a committed, engaged student body excited to contribute to creative projects, learn in the real world, and explore the classroom in the public sphere.

Working within an academic setting also raises questions: How exactly do we evaluate projects that cross disciplines and communities? Students, researchers, locals, and artist collaborators who are all involved in circles of participation often become both participant and audience. Which communities are seen as participants in these projects and which as audience? How are these various communities drawn into engagement, and who evaluates the success of these projects (if not the primary audiences)?

What follows are a selection of SPARC-supported projects describing the breadth of creative approaches and methods of civic, pedagogical and social engagement. SPARC invites artist fellows to create projects that address sites, issues, or communities that have relevance to the local environment in and around Santa Cruz. Artists work in collaboration with SPARC over a period of two years producing a project. At the same time, the projects are involved in fundraising, site investigations, and community building. SPARC also works with artist affiliates who create projects that have a focus outside of the local area but whose work has significance to the UCSC and the City of Santa Cruz.

LISTENING AS SOCIAL PRACTICE: A PEDAGOGY OF THE EAR

In 2014, SPARC invited the sound art collective Ultra Red to be SPARC artist fellows. Ultra Red members worked with the support of UCSC professors and a group of UCSC students. Ultra Red held a series of workshops titled "Listening as Social Practice: a Pedagogy of the Ear," which coincided with contract negotiations at UC for the teaching assistants union, including two strikes that shut down the university. The strikes, and arrest of some student strikers, were highly impactful on many of the students participating in the project.

Ultra Red facilitated a series of "listening sessions" with students, a term the collective uses to describe a series of protocols for careful listening to audio samples that they refer to as "sound objects." By focusing critical attention on both the content of what participants hear and on the act of listening itself, Ultra Red transforms listening into their artistic medium. For many students, the labor action was their first experience with collective political organizing. During feedback sessions students vigorously debated whether it is valuable to learn from outsiders when one is involved in a collaboration or political movement. The intensity of their conversation proved this subject to be a critical issue for the group to explore. What emerged very quickly from the group was a diffused understanding of solidarity among students. In smaller groups, students analyzed definitions of solidarity. These conversations led to a constellation of themes around solidarity and the role of the outsider as informer, which were then offered back to the group as the basis for field recordings to be conducted by students.

A listening session was held in the middle of UCSC's Porter College campus with research teams presenting short sound objects. Each sound object was followed by an invitation for anyone to approach and respond to the question "What did you hear?" speaking into microphones and writing their thoughts on paper. Once all of the recordings had been played, the entire group was invited to reflect freely on the process. These meetings involved processing the entire experience but also teasing out how and in what ways the sound investigation process might have a use in the actual context of social justice organizations and collectives. This experience became the basis for the final meetings with students.

Ultra Red's project focused specifically on students around an issue that directly impacted the participants. The final sound objects were performed for an audience of passersby, yet clearly the real benefactors of the experience were the students involved in creating the sound objects themselves. The work became both representation and lived experience for the participants, who themselves became the audience for the work. This shows how a community of students can be engaged in a meaningful way.

BUILDING STORIES

Students and graduates at UCSC frequently have a strong interest in the cultivation of local community relationships. Their commitment to civic engagement and dialogue with local communities creates rich and complex dynamics within the city itself. One recent example of a project supported by SPARC is the building collective's project *Building Stories*, which utilizes the methodologies of ethnographic practice: fieldwork, cultural mapping, and personal history to articulate a local identity beyond the packaged tourism of Santa Cruz. *Building Stories* solicited secret histories of Santa Cruz from residents collected through workshops, dialogues, and loosely facilitated group discussions. The building collective reached out to potential participants via email and social media through organizations such as Barrios Unidos, Free Skool Santa Cruz, and Researchers Anonymous. Building collective members walked the streets of neighborhoods on the morning preceding workshops, talking to passersby and knocking on doors with invitations.

Participants were invited to share memories and reflect on historical insights that might inform solutions to civic and social problems that Santa Cruz currently faces. Participants willingly contributed stories, describing recollections of being locked up in the county jail in the protests against the war in Vietnam, stories of fruit trees that they used to glean food from and of quarries that have since become suburban housing tracts. The building collective gathered these stories through note taking, interviews, and worksheets. Wall-sized "concept maps" were created on the walls of the Museum of Art and History in Santa Cruz, an amalgam of cartographic maps and diagrammatic renderings of the secret histories contributed by participants.

LINEAGE: MATCHMAKING IN THE ARCHIVE

Not all SPARC projects tie directly to students or are focused locally. The center also endorses creative projects that explore and define community in relation to identity rather than locale. For example, one professor's projects explore and create archives that preserve lesbian, gay, bisexual, and transgender histories. This project resulted in the creation of *Lineage: Matchmaking in the Archive*, in which the professor matched a living person with the archive of an individual in the Gay Lesbian Bisexual Transgender Historical Society. The body of creative work to emerge from this process became a part of the archives itself and has since traveled across national and international borders.

LARGE-SCALE COLLABORATIONS

SPARC has been involved with two large-scale projects from the nascent stages. These projects are the brainchild of Barbara Benish, founding director of the non-governmental organization (NGO) Art Dialogue, who is working to create the SS Palo Alto project, and Janeil Englestad, founding director of MAP—Make Art with a Purpose. Their projects function as organizational hubs bringing communities of artists together with communities and specialists. Through civic engagement in the public sphere, they are creating tangible changes in local communities. Both artists work in collaboration with a complex mix of funders, NGOs, government agencies and others. SPARC's affiliation with these artists and their projects is ongoing, evolving as their projects grow to national significance.

For this chapter I invited the artists to describe their projects and define their strategies for vibrant civic engagement.

ART DIALOGUE AND THE SS PALO ALTO PROJECT, BY BARBARA BENISH

> Artists are Placemakers: when you bring arts organizations and arts workers into a neighborhood, the place changes to a vibrant and sustainable community.[1]

In 2012, Dr. Jane Lubchenco, then under-secretary of commerce for oceans and atmosphere at the National Oceanic and Atmospheric Administration, stated that one of the largest difficulties facing conservation and protection of the oceans is not just budget but cross-semination of information. The SS Palo Alto project is a creative attempt to bridge this gap between information and public in inspiring new ways to utilize the power of creativity in the public sphere to enact real change around ocean sustainability.

As a SPARC artist fellow from 2012 to 2014 at UCSC, I was able to develop this project from a grassroots perspective. The SS Palo Alto project proposed the creation of an art park, an aesthetically enhanced public space surrounding a derelict military ship on the central coast of California, designed to engage transformative education, inspire environmental awareness, and promote ocean sustainability. The seeds of this project were planted in collaboration with the local communities at Seacliff State Park, UCSC students, the Cal State University system, the 5Gyres Institute, and the United Nations Safe Planet Campaign, as well as several world-renowned marine labs that circle the Monterey Bay Sanctuary.

The SS Palo Alto is a cultural and historical landmark along the Monterey Bay, beloved by generations of fishermen, tourists, and locals alike, already laden with cultural meaning: the ship's WWI military history, her unique concrete construction and engineering, the ship's romantic history as a converted ballroom and bootlegging hall during the roaring 1920s, and now the cement ship's (as she is colloquially called) eminent transformation into an underwater reef, teaming with a rich marine eco-system. Repurposing the ship to an art park involves engaging the local community that lives there and visits her every day.

This project is a vast and complex one, intended to build and grow over the next decade. What follows is a description of the public engagement strategies I have been developing through the SS Palo Alto project, based on similar large-scale projects in Prague, Dallas, and Los Angeles over the past several decades.

The SS Palo Alto project models ways the arts can engage communities in sustainable development around the world, by creating public spaces that transform the social contract. Krystof Wodiczko describes two of the central challenges in public art: that of (1) critical discourse between the inhabitants themselves and the environment and (2) creating an aesthetic practice that makes existing symbolic structures respond to contemporary events.[2] In the case of the SS Palo Alto project, this translates to reframing an already popular landmark into an aesthetically inspired site that engages the public with the ocean in more than just a romantic cliché of a sinking ship at sunset. Artworks and engaging activities embedded on the site transform the experience of the viewer and how they respond to the surrounding space in terms of climate change, ocean acidification and plastic pollution.

To that end, the SS Palo Alto project started with community meetings, presentations at local civic groups and commerce organizations in Sea Cliff, lectures at the local university, and outreach to the public. Through public events at the ship and pier, we have engaged students of all ages and passersby in parades and beanbag tosses, games, and beach cleanups geared toward children as well as adults. Shared activities at the site were intended to create interest and dialogue, all based on themes of ocean

Figure 8.1.   SS Palo Alto

conservation and awareness: plastic pollution, derelict fishing gear and marine debris, and science experiments based on studying the marine mammal life surrounding and living on the ship or on the beach. All of these activities set up the critical discourse that Wodizko refers to, thus creating a dialogue and potential for change.

Besides engaging the public, any successful public art project must reach out to similar organizations and create broad-based partnerships. To this end the SS Palo Alto project works with Save Our Shores, the 5Gyres Institute, Marine Long Lab, Fish Wise, the local restaurants and Snack Shack at the beach, as well as several other ocean conservancy groups of the Monterey Bay region. We have developed outreach programs at the ship to illustrate how toxins enter our bodies and the sea. In addition, the project engages local middle schools by running art contests on ocean themes and working on curriculum development on ocean sustainability issues and art with the massive California State University system, alongside international partnerships with the United Nations Environment Programme, and the local California Regional Environmental Education Community. This broad spectrum of engagement aims to provide local, regional, and international structures of support, which is a necessary framework for such an ambitious public works project that breaks traditional definitions of art, science, and education. These are also partnerships that help to build a funding base for grants, donations, and resource-creating events.

The task of setting up an aesthetic practice was part of the second phase. Once the public and financial support was in place, artists created works to be displayed and installed in and near the site itself. Many of these local and international artists work in time-based, performative, or otherwise interactive art forms that engage the public on an aesthetic level beyond traditional sculpture parks. It is intended that works will rotate yearly, some will be permanent, but many will change and renew like an exhibition. It is here that artworks have the potential to engage in educational and transformative marine curriculum for the thousands of visitors and students who come to Seacliff State Park each year.

How can a public be engaged in the United States, sitting in an affluent community by the seaside, changing a lifestyle that is comfortable, "affordable," and reenforced by the advertising and media machines at every waking moment? Seacliff State Park, like many California beaches, is the one public sphere where diverse races and classes meet. Visitors to the ship are foreign tourists (estimated at four million a year), Latino families on the weekends, and white locals in jogging clothes walking dogs and exchanging greetings each morning. The social mix is more in the summer, often swelling to hundreds of thousands on holiday weekends. It is a meeting place for education, outreach, and inspiration on the discrepancies of consumption, foreign import, and waste among various ethnic and social groups. It is a local project with global potential, creating social and political change as the ship sinks into the sea over the coming generation. Or, more correctly, the sea level is rising around her hull, and the public can visualize climate change while walking along the shore.

MAP—MAKE ART WITH PURPOSE: BUILDING RELATIONSHIPS AND INITIATING CHANGE, BY JANEIL ENGLESTAD

In the last decade, artists are increasingly abandoning the studio to develop creative practices that address social and environmental needs with the objective of positive change. In the process, they are creating new models for public art that engage citizens as cocreators. They are employing cross-disciplinary collaboration and expertise. In addition, they are forging alliances with small and large organizations in the public and private sector to help fund, organize, and support their projects. Unfortunately, the professional activity undertaken by artists working in this way is often organized outside of formal networks, and as a result, the work is not valued as a part of the process of creating public art. For this reason, I founded, MAP—Make Art with Purpose in part to catalyze and organize various stakeholders into productive partnerships that realize the potential and value of public art and other projects that generally fall under the realm of social practice.[3] MAP conceives and initiates its own projects and also collaborates with artists and organizations to help bring to fruition their visions for public art that concurs with MAP's mission.

MAP public art programs are designed with an underlying spirit of reciprocity between artists, administrators, participants, and funders. In each location where a project takes place there is on-the-ground flexibility to allow for unexpected and spontaneous community input and involvement and an ecology that accounts for and honors local knowledge and cultural norms. To accomplish this, MAP begins each project with community gatherings, or meetings of the participants, where everyone is invited to share their creative ideas and goals. It is the job of the artist and/or project director to orchestrate this input into a cohesive, inclusive plan that also takes into account the project budget and aesthetics. Leadership is an important skill for this work. One needs to ensure that each of the participants is recognized, heard, and valued. The leader must guide the participants toward compromise and the letting go of unrealistic ideas while striving, in the end, for excellence. Each MAP public art project includes workshops with exercises that involve cooperation, dialogue, and the teaching of skills that promote individual and collective growth. The primary underpinning that holds up this mission and platform is collaboration. Working with NGOs, government agencies, foundations, grassroots community organizations and partners, such as SPARC at UCSC, MAP is able to realize a scale of production and measurable change that would not be possible if the organization were acting alone.

Collaboration and dependency on outside donors carries the danger of an external agenda hijacking a project, thus MAP projects engage a variety of forces, including, social, economic, cultural, political, ecological, and aesthetic to develop and produce its work. This helps to establish an active space where artists can create work in a collaborative, productive environment that is thoughtfully cultivated and tended. These resources and networks provide inspiration and support as well as sharing and exchange of ideas.

Through collaboration, MAP is helping to create and be a part of an extensive international network of creative thinkers and change makers. It is also a laboratory for cross-media and cross-cultural practices, often incorporating new technologies and tools for innovative art making and design. Technology is a tool not only for creating art but also for sharing plans and ideas with communities around the world that are looking to replicate similar projects. MAP distributes this information through traditional means, such as its website and printed materials. Additionally, to reach people in remote locations who do not have access to computers or the internet, MAP uses Open Data Kit to reach people on cell phones. The sharing of methodologies and ideas is built into every project. Designed as a part of the material outcome, these models and plans are an integral piece of the public art.

MAP 2013

Merging ideas and methodologies from social practice and public art, MAP created a large-scale project in 2013 throughout the greater Dallas–Fort Worth area, titled *MAP 2013: Projects That Restore and Preserve the Environment, Promote Social Justice and Advance Human Knowledge and Well-Being.* Over thirty programs and projects were produced for *MAP 2013*, engaging the community as active participants while promoting new approaches and models for public art, for social practice, and for creating and maintaining public space. *MAP 2013* built connections and relationships between local and regional, national and international artists and organizations. This structure allowed for expansive viewpoints and an exchange of experience and knowledge, but in some instances also created challenges between participants.

Instrument for Listening is part of Oto Hudec's international body of work that explores immigration and migration. Hudec's *MAP 2013* public sculpture, *Instrument for Listening*, would not have been possible without collaboration with Dallas's Latino community members and the participation of over a half-dozen partner organizations, each coming to the project with a different agenda. The sculpture, a giant working megaphone constructed of plywood and decorated with symbols that represented the Latino community, broadcast portions of Hudec's interviews with Latinos about their lives, their dreams, and their views on immigration. The symbols were developed and painted onto the megaphone by Hispanic youth from Dallas middle schools. Coming to the project as an outsider, Hudec's purpose was to understand the Latino immigrant experience beyond the viewpoints that he was reading in the media.

As the Dallas project progressed, one partner organization wanted to shape and claim the project as its own, creating tension in the larger cohort. Work on the project was put on hold to allow time for the various stakeholders to communicate and work out competing agendas. This was successful in part because the project had a generous timeline that anticipated potential problems with construction, permits, site prep, and communication. *Instrument for Listening* was installed for four

Figure 8.2.   Marriators and translators

months in a popular public park on Main Street in downtown Dallas. It provided a communication platform for Dallas community members whose voices are rarely represented in the mainstream media.

Instrument for Listening was launched simultaneously with another *MAP 2013* project, *Translating Culture . . . Community Voices at the Dallas Museum of Art*. Taking place over several months, and during a time when the DMA was in the process of embracing new ideas for engaging the community (and returning to free general admission), the foundation of *Translating Culture* was a series of workshops that took place twice a week where eleven members of the Dallas chapter of AVANCE (a national nonprofit dedicated to providing innovative education and family support services to Latino families), learned about the DMA's collections.

Working independently, in pairs, and as a group, the participants wrote their personal interpretations about a work of art of their choice. Their texts, along with images of the selected art, were included in the DMA's first ever bilingual Spanish and English printed guide for visitors. Over the summer, as *Translating Culture* continued, the participants took ownership of the museum and its collections. This made them feel comfortable and at home in a place that some of them had not visited before the outset of the project. They, in turn, have invited and brought their families and friends to the museum, expanding the project to include an ever-widening circle of community members.

Through *Translating Culture* and *Instrument for Listening*, MAP realized a core part of its mission, which is to produce public art and other programs that are inclusive of multiple voices and perspectives and to provide access to cultural programs for communities that are often marginalized because of ethnicity and socioeconomic reasons. Launching these two programs simultaneously created a media storm and a larger city—wide conversation about the experience of the Hispanic community living in North Texas. These conversations have continued into additional MAP projects, including murals created by Latino youth that illustrate immigration and local Hispanic history. It organized community discussions about the relationship between Latinos, African Americans, Caucasians, and people from other ethnicities living in Dallas.

As communities throughout the world become increasingly interconnected through technology and around issues such as human rights and climate change, innovative partnerships between organizations are fundamental to helping cities and towns create public art that is inclusive, builds communities, and creates cohesiveness. Enhancing civic engagement through participatory public art projects that includes multigenerational groups of people from different racial backgrounds and ethnicities produces unique opportunities for artists, cultural institutions, government agencies, and other individuals and organizations to collaborate, build relationships, and increase understanding that benefits the collective whole.

CONCLUSION

The artist projects described in this chapter have an investment in the public sphere as a place of learning, teaching, and active engagement, of civic debate and active participation. The power of community is a central component of these practices. Whether the primary audience is an expert in marine biology, a student, or a migrant worker, each individual becomes an honored expert in their own experience, an active participant and citizen in the project, no longer a passive spectator merely witnessing but a key part of the creative process whose contribution to the project is itself a learning and teaching opportunity.

NOTES

1. Ann McQueen, "An Interview with Rocco Landesman Chairman, National Endowment for the Arts," *Grantmakers in the Arts Reader* 24, no. 1 (Winter 2013).

2. Krzysztof Wodiczko, "Projections," *Perspecta: Theatre, Theatricality, and Architecture*, no. 26 (1990): 273.

3. The type of art referred to as "social practice" includes art made to draw awareness to or have an impact on a social issue or concern and participatory art, where the audience engages in the production of the piece, often with the objective of community empowerment. The social interaction that the artist undertakes to produce the work is a part of the art.

9

Grandmother's Kitchen/ Grandfather's Garden

Growing Art and Culture in City Heights

Nigel Brookes

INTRODUCTION

This chapter attempts to evoke and represent how art binds seemingly distinct civic practices into an organic whole, an engaged community. Specifically, it looks at how public art[1] is working in the San Diego community of City Heights, told through the voices of its resident artists and activists to reveal how the distinction between those two roles is blurred in their own lives. It identifies and makes explicit through representations of artistic/activist experiences the fertile ecology of relationships working within a framework of nonprofit and governmental support for a traditionally underserved community suffering from a history of great struggles, within which this art was created and is now situated. This is a community in a self-conscious state of becoming, already using, leveraging, and adapting various types of support, including but not limited to art, to become self-determining. In general, the chapter is about how a lack of economic affluence can catalyze the development of cultural and aesthetic affluence when civic and private stakeholders exert their will toward accomplishing that end. Furthermore, this increased cultural abundance provides a value that is different in nature than economic value but no less existentially significant for the people of the neighborhood.

Although our complex culture tends toward policies that centralize the acquisition and redistribution of resources in the service of predictable outcomes, art's relationship to civic life presents a mercurial dynamic, as evidenced by the intersecting stories of City Heights. The efficacy of public artworks in this community results from established, interdependent relationships and the shared interests of its residents and cultural producers. Many of the art practices that connect this community have emerged organically, from the ground up, and in response to directly experienced needs. The immediacy of these needs takes the form of pain: from the

Figure 9.1. City Heights Community Garden
Photo by Anna Daniels

former lives its many refugees are fleeing, from a traditional lack of resources and support, from the displacement of thousands who lived and worked where the larger culture wanted a freeway. A rationale for focusing on this type of story and presenting it through the participants' voices is encouraged by Joshua Guetzkow's identification of a gap in public art literature: "Researchers studying the impact of the arts are rarely sensitive to contextual or intervening factors that influence the outcomes they find . . . it is likely that impact[s] vary depending on the size of the community under discussion and the size and density of arts organizations/events."[2] Because the art to be discussed is in a highly dynamic community, unique in many aspects, it is this context that first needs describing.

THE CONTEXT

City Heights is a vibrant urban community three miles east of downtown San Diego consisting of sixteen defined neighborhoods. Approximately 75,000 people reside in 23,827 households with over 38,000 under thirty years of age, all within a four-square-mile area, making it the most densely populated community in the San Diego region. Over 40 percent of residents are foreign born, and only 63 percent of adults have a high school diploma.[3] With a median income of $35,776, families within City Heights live on just more than half the countywide median income of $63,373.[4]

In the last four decades, the City of San Diego has become a hub for the re-settlement of refugees fleeing wars and conflict around the world, from Vietnam to Somalia to Iraq. Many have settled in City Heights. In 2013 alone, according to local resettlement workers, about five thousand refugees arrived in San Diego, leading some local refugee advocates to call San Diego the refugee capital of the United States.[5] The International Rescue Committee[6] (IRC) program in San Diego manages the housing and support for refugees coming to City Heights. The IRC got its start in 1975 relocating tens of thousands of Vietnamese refugees from nearby Camp Pendleton Marine Base to City Heights and other affordable areas.[7]

In 1994 Sol Price, founder of The Price Club, which eventually became Costco, first became philanthropically interested in focusing his efforts in City Heights as a result of a newspaper article about a community performance art piece presented as a funeral with a casket to protest a chain grocery store closing in the community. At this time City Heights had the highest crime rate in San Diego County.[8] During this same year, while Price began funding civic improvements, an approximately seven-mile section of freeway was built, connecting freeways to the north and south while razing a one-mile strip of homes and businesses in this community. "On the drawing board since 1959—postponed due to the energy crisis, inflation of the 1970s and increasing property costs in San Diego, Caltrans began telling residents as early as 1965 that construction was imminent and encouraged affected property owners to not improve properties in the construction zone, exacerbating blight."[9] Social research has shown highway construction has had "devastating consequences on lower-income, minority, inner-city neighborhoods, which were politically powerless to prevent such impacts."[10] In 1991, after Caltrans razed over 1,100 residences and businesses along

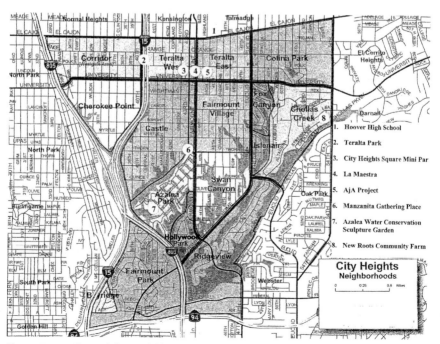

Figure 9.2.   City Heights Neighborhoods

eight blocks of 40th Street and displaced over 4,000 people in preparation for the freeway, community activists received permission to create a one-acre community garden on the site, which lasted five years until the freeway construction.[11]

As a way of recreating this agriculturally oriented gathering space, in 2007 the IRC established the award-winning New Roots Community Farm, which provides growing spaces for eighty-five families one and a half miles east of the freeway, still within City Heights. They were motivated by an understanding that many of the participants were farmers in their home countries and this is their first opportunity to reconnect with the land in the United States, as well as double their family's food security and nutrition access.[12] The farm is also open to the public.

As a native San Diegan and a lifelong art maker, City Heights and its residents have been an integral part of my adult life. When I was younger, I drove a taxi in that part of town when it had the highest crime rate in the county, even getting robbed at the time. Through friends and acquaintances, I was poignantly aware of the disruption the freeway project brought to the community. And I have witnessed the emergence of grassroots community cohesion in the time since. Through managing the two City of San Diego public art projects described in this chapter and participating in the Pomegranate Fellowship that reclaimed a blighted City Heights lot, I was fortunate to build strong relationships with the resident leaders of this community. It is from that point of view that I reached out to hear the stories of the people who are actively working to steward and nurture this ongoing project of community cohesion.

Figure 9.3.   New Roots Community Farm[13]

During its construction, many members of the community felt the freeway project to be a metaphoric as well as literal wound through its heart.[14] And some, including City Heights resident artist and director of the Center for Urban Economics and Design Jim Bliesner, organized to achieve some degree of remedy. Although Bliesner earned a degree in philosophy of social ethics from Boston University, he had always painted, a practice he refined while attending an art-centric high school. As part of his interest in applying the abstract ideas of social ethics to everyday life, Jim moved to the Azalea Park neighborhood in City Heights with his young family in 1975 to work as a community organizer. He supported his family as an oil painter while continuing his education in the day-to-day work of activism, founding the CHCDC (City Heights Community Development Corporation)[15] in 1980. He discovered a relationship between his two vocations in that they both required "being conscious and intentional like an artist and like a community organizer."[16] By the late 1980s, the disruption and displacement of his community by the freeway construction constituted what Bliesner considered the largest single fragmentation of his neighborhood. He discovered in his research that Environmental Impact Studies included "Neighborhood Cohesion," a factor that could be used for receiving some degree of institutional mitigation. Bliesner worked with the CHCDC and other neighborhood stakeholders and, through that coalition, received a grant for $150,000 to hire the architects that designed the Big Dig underground freeway project in Boston. "We did a huge community engagement process and had thousands of people participate in the design. We had our architects give Caltrans a design for the cover of the entire freeway and presented it to the city council."[17] Their struggle was only partially successful; the freeway would be only partially covered. As an activist from that time reports, "the costs per square foot could not be justified—in City Heights."[18] But even a partial success was deemed a victory by the activists. Jim had come to see the landscaped freeway cover—named Teralta Park—as a blend of community art and activism. "I began to see the conceptualization of the solution to the negative effects of the freeway as a piece of conceptual art. I'd take friends and we'd go stand on the cover of the freeway and I'd say this was my greatest piece of conceptual art."[19]

In 1992, shortly before the freeway's construction, the French American public artist Niki de Saint Phalle moved to San Diego to be near state of the art medical care for her lungs, damaged after years of exposure to toxic fumes from the chemicals she used in her work. After plans for the Teralta Park highway cover were approved, Congresswoman Susan Davis approached Saint Phalle, internationally and locally famous for her large-scale mosaic works, and asked her to contribute art for that site. Saint Phalle's initial proposal directed her charitable art foundation to donate *La Cabeza*, an enormous Day of the Dead skull, to be crawled on by children and containing an interior meditation chamber—as well as $25,000 to install and maintain the artwork. Although grateful, community leaders voted to not receive the artwork because they feared it would become an attractive target for vandals. Instead, she agreed to donate the money anyway and have it earmarked for the creation of a new public artwork, designed in a manner and installed in a location deemed appropriate by the community. According to her business manager David Stevenson, Saint Phalle was inspired by the story of City Heights and hoped her donation would produce artwork that would serve as a balm for the wound of the freeway, based on her strong faith that art can heal. Unfortunately Saint Phalle died before a suitable public art opportunity was identified for her donation. However, in keeping with Saint Phalle's intention to create art as a healing agent, the City of San Diego, in May 2009, put out a call for artists crafted to reflect the story and struggle of City Heights, stating: "*Witnessing the geographical and social bifurcation of the City Heights neighborhood during the construction of Interstate 15, Niki developed a* particular concern about the well-being of the community in this area of San Diego. She envisioned public art as a healing force for the neighborhood."[20] Further, it specifically sought artists "to create permanent, documentary public artwork(s) such as drawings, paintings, prints, photographs, videos or multimedia artworks, which record the unique nature of City Heights and engender community."[21] The artist selection panel included Saint Phalle's business manager, David Stevenson; geographically relevant city council staff; the project facilitator for the City Heights–based AjA Project;[22] and other community leaders. Utilizing artist evaluation criteria such as evidence of original vision, sophisticated conceptual skills, demonstrated understanding of the project, and strength of the artist's expressed methods for engendering community, the panel selected Lynn Susholtz. She had an established reputation as a successful local public artist, educator, and community activist in City Heights and surrounding neighborhoods.

GRANDMOTHER'S KITCHEN/GRANDFATHER'S GARDEN

The project appealed to Susholtz on several levels, not the least of which was her interest in Saint Phalle as a source of inspiration. "She was one of my superheroes as a kid. There weren't too many women artists that I knew of. One of my other heroes was her husband, Tinguely. That was a beautiful full-circle kind of thing."[23] Susholtz acknowledged the significance of the "documentary" art-making framework and described it as being an important component in her interest in the project and her creative process. "I think once you know the direction of a piece is to represent a neighborhood in some way and tell a story of a neighborhood, then you have to kind of be embedded in that neighborhood and engaged in the community to have it make sense."[24]

For Susholtz, she understood that her established relationships were a strength she brought to the process, one that offered her "a jumpstart on the research phase," from the work she had been doing "in the community for a number of years, in the schools and arts organizations based there."[25] Part of that previous work included her project *Mapping the Hood*, funded through a San Diego Foundation[26] community engagement program. She describes the experience as a "crazy, in-depth, yearlong collaboration between me, two dance companies, and architectural grad students exploring and documenting the neighborhood."[27] The project paired community members with the architectural students to perform spatial and cultural research on every city street block within the mapping. The work resulted in a spoken-word/ video performance piece that ran for a month as well as yearlong, monthly, free public engagement workshops.

Another project by Susholtz involved working at local Hoover High School with students and staff on an environmental design intervention in their administrative offices to do physical facade improvements to the exterior of the building. These projects further educated Susholtz about the diverse and changing makeup of City Heights. She had worked in the classroom with "33 students from 15 countries speaking 57 language groups. I mean, it was like little United Nations in this classroom and in some of these apartment buildings. So, I always knew the story I wanted to tell about City Heights."[28]

During the research phase for the artwork, she brought the kids and their families that she was connected with to Art Produce,[29] her studio, gallery, and urban garden. "You know, that's where we would tell our stories, and that's what they would share, the cultural knowledge from their tribes and villages or the leaves of the squash where they came from."[30] The inspiration and evolution of her art piece resulted from "getting more involved in the project and working with the students and their families over a period of about four years and the connection that we all had through food and farming. It was a moment of recognizing how we share and contain and embody our history through our food . . . our culturally specific foods."[31]

Susholtz had been impressed by the City Heights Farmers Market that began in 2008 as a location for cultural and entrepreneurial synergy, with musicians, drummers, and local crafts people. She began to see her richly diverse community and their food ways as a type of "cultural-based knowledge" that she could "share with other people and other communities . . . the fact that it's not a monoculture like many of our communities." And she sees these connections as part of what calls her to practice art in this community. "That's what makes me excited about communities like City Heights, you know, there's still so much opportunity to create the place and participate in the building of it and the forming of it. There's still plenty of room, and it's not just about decorating it."[32] Susholtz wanted her art to embody the community she works with and represent what she came to appreciate as its character.

To this end, *Grandmother's Kitchen/Grandfather's Garden* was created, an acrylic sculpture of locally grown vegetables, inset with three video monitors showing various citizens of City Heights engaged in growing and preparing food. Often wearing clothing specific to their homelands, the participants are seen preparing traditional foods and using traditional tools they brought with them. During this time, the economy had crashed and services and hours of operation were being drastically cut, constraining the access to the art the public might have in government-owned facilities, such as libraries. Susholtz, thus, proposed to install her art in La Maestra because it had longer hours of operation.[33] La Maestra is a private, nonprofit outpatient health center providing quality health care and support services to low income, uninsured, and underserved populations throughout San Diego. La Maestra meets the needs of the increasing influx of foreign-born refugees and immigrants into City Heights and serves ninety thousand countywide patients annually. It was founded by CEO Zara Marselian twenty-four years ago, which then operated out of a City Heights apartment complex. They have expanded greatly over the years by building strong relationships within the communities they serve and with institutional support from groups such as Price Charities, which helped them open their flagship thirty-thousand-square-foot La Maestra Community Health Centers—City Heights on Fairmount Avenues in August 2010. Part of the expansion in service to the community is the recently implemented Culture and Healing through Art (CHA)[34] program in the clinic where Susholtz's artwork was the inaugural piece. Still in an implementation phase, additional art for the CHA will be curated from works brought by immigrant and refugee communities and donated to the clinic as well as art created in their own art classes. The city, through its arts commission, aware of and sensitive to the community's needs, agreed to support this solution. For Susholtz, "it ended up being a perfect site for it." She added, "I worked with the staff at La Maestra, who are excited to see their community's culture represented and to create healthy nutritional examples for food in this country."[35]

The CHA program was partially inspired by an established art therapy program La Maestra has been managing for some years. Marselian remembers adolescent participants "putting their feelings on rocks and painting them. You could see the teens were sitting there talking about their emotions; they're telling you their whole story."[36] And that became the inspiration to initiate after school/summer art classes. Marselian wanted the youth in her programs to understand La Maestra recognized them as special, which she considers facilitating "collective well-being." Her increasing commitment to art emerged from her focus on promoting community health, and, as such, her art programming is always presented within a context of health care, which strategically connects the art to "coaching and mentoring, building self-confidence, giving the community a safe place to hang out and learn about good nutrition and exercise."[37] According to Marselian, one of the benefits of so much art in an underserved community is

> that means the community isn't so focused 100 percent on just survival needs. Now you can take a minute and concentrate on some of the more intrinsic components of wellness. Art is one of them. I would say that through self-expression, and being able to have a minute to do that—and the resources to do that—indicates that basic needs are being met, or, at least, they are available as resources in the community.[38]

Marselian recalls consultants she worked with during the building of her clinic taking her on tours to see how art was used in other, established health-care facilities. She interpreted the experience as essentially being told, "We're going to take you to five different places so you can see what art is and so you get a good education about art."[39] However, she found the art on her tours "super sterile [artwork] that doesn't look like anything that is representative of this population."[40] That experience informed her receptivity to Susholtz's proposal of installing art in her clinic. "So when Lynn came along with this project—Hallelujah!—she got it. She paid attention to the community. She paid attention to who's here."[41] She recognized in Susholtz a fellow "stakeholder" in the City Heights community, someone who like herself wanted to honor the diverse traditions people brought to the community and to effectively integrate them. "She was very receptive, and she got it. You could tell."[42]

CITY HEIGHTS SQUARE MINI PARK

The La Maestra Community Health Centers–City Heights, where Susholtz's piece is installed, is one of many capital projects built by Price Charities,[43] a real estate development nonprofit, formally established by Sol and his wife, Helen, in 2000—along with Price Philanthropies, a grant-making foundation—to support City Heights in a focused and consistent manner. Matthew Hervey is the Community Development Director for Price Charities. He was recruited in the formative stages when Sol Price was still looking for a community he could "wrap his arms around,"[44] an area of sufficiently small scale that his concentrated investments might have significant impact. Hervey reports their primary function is to identify already existing nonprofits, determine what they do well, and help them perform even better. An example of the charity's commitment to art and its willingness to take a hand in innovating how that shows up in the community is a piece they had created for the 5,400–square-foot City Heights Square Mini Park, another real estate project, operated by the city's Parks and Recreation Department and contiguous with the land on which La Maestra sits.

Hervey was actively involved in that project and feels pride in its fruition. They put out a call for bids from local artists, and AjA Project came back with the best proposal. It resulted in a digital photographic tile mural installed on the back wall of a Price-owned building that abuts the park. The portrait imagery on each of the tiles was created by AjA students, and the organization and installation of the work was managed by one of their lead artists. This work is, thus, another example of "documentary" and community art—a piece that reflects the members of the community, created by those very members. Hervey reflects:

> I think that's a theme of the community. It's very much an activist community where they are shaping it to reflect an identification they want; that they're building their own community, we're merely trying to help facilitate that. Art has to give people pride in their community. It has to give relevance to the community. It has to contribute. Just putting something there to just be there isn't the purpose of what we are doing.[45]

When it comes to art-specific projects, Price doesn't directly manage the process. They trust the nonprofits with which they have established relationships to use their networks and skill sets. It embodies the organizational vision described by Price

Charities Executive Vice President Jack McGrory: "We created the shell so that other people could come along and help deliver the services along with us."[46] For the mural, AjA Project did the outreach to the students and area residents, gave them disposable cameras, and had them take portraits of themselves and friends.

Within this same park, another City of San Diego public artwork was installed on the iron fence on the park's western entrance. Native San Diegan and art professor Wendell Kling created his first public art work for the Price Charities–funded city park. After two community meetings and presenting his initial proposal, Kling went back to the proverbial and literal drawing board to account for a small minority that didn't like a minor aspect of his images. After several weeks of walking and riding his bike around City Heights, Kling's second design was met at the next community meeting with unanimous approval, a Plexiglas® and metal stencil depicting animals indigenous to the community's canyons and the plants and tools of the many urban gardens he observed on his walks. Kling saw a connection between the practice of urban farming in City Heights and his own home practice which, along with biking, he calls, "his two extant political acts."[47] Through the process of close observation, in the manner of a "permaculturist,"[48] he chose to reflect what he saw working in City Heights, because "gardening is a way of making the world a better place by degrees."[49] Kling reports being pleased to have his artwork watched over by the AjA Project mural.

The AjA Project mural is just a few hundred feet from the AjA Project headquarters, where its executive director, Sandra Ainslie, manages the OSP-funded[50] organization. Ainslie was raised in San Diego in a bicultural, bilingual family with members living and working on both sides of the Mexican/American border. This dynamic inspired her to become a cultural anthropologist by education and a documentary photographer as her artistic vocation, both of which inform her process of studying the "intersection between identity and community and how that gets shaped."[51] She began artistic projects of photographing local nonprofits, and then her interests evolved into international work, traveling to photograph child soldiers in Uganda. It was while working in a rehabilitation center in Northern Uganda that she had an epiphany.

> I was photographing them and they were giving me the same sort of thing over and over and over, which is the part of their identity they knew I was there to capture, the "I've been through trauma. I've lost all semblance of self, of family. I've committed and seen atrocity." So that is what they were giving me, these portraits of this very empty, vacant, sad sort of souls.[52]

The children wanted to play with her camera, and so she gave it to them.

> What I noticed was that when they were photographing each other, they shifted their identity. They suddenly were acting out versions of themselves that they were hopeful to become. The girls were pretending to hold babies and be nurturing mothers. The boys were pretending to be soccer players.[53]

To Ainslie, it was crystal clear. "If you give someone the power to represent themselves, they represent the best that they can be, their aspirational self."[54] It is a sentiment reflected in the artist statement of Nick Beda, a Sudanese refugee and AjA student whose work was on display in their main gallery: "I have learned that if you don't tell people who you are and where you come from, they will think and tell you where they believe you fit in." AjA's art/activist model is "participatory photography," designed to get people to find their aspirations and become "change agents" in realizing that process.

Alternately, Ainslie sees her organization and others already working in her neighborhood as establishing projects that "bring [residents] together in the way that gives them ownership over the process and the product,"[55] not in a perfunctory way but in a manner that identifies their perceived needs and holds a conversation around what meeting those needs can look like.

For example, we don't say to young people, "Hey, there's a lack of green space in your community. Why don't you do something about it?" We just say, "Observe what's happening around you and then reflect on your own well-being and needs. What are you observing both externally and internally? And who can you be in this situation?" Ultimately, they'll arrive at "You know, there's a lack of green space. I would feel happier if I could see pretty flowers when I walk to school."[56]

She acknowledges such a distinction may seem minimal at an abstract level but notes that through this type of process "a thirteen-year-old student from Monroe Clark Middle School initiated a community garden project to plant flowers on the walk to school and a garden at school."[57] And this initiating process is how she sees "ownership" and "change agency" emerging in the work they do. Ainslie strives to work with other organizations in the community that share these values and thus has disseminated invitations to some of the canyon work projects immediately to her south in City Heights' Azalea Park, even sending her students to observe and photograph the work that people in those groups are doing.

AZALEA PARK CANYONS: ECOLOGY AND ART

Linda Pennington is regarded by many in City Heights as a primary nexus for various organizational networks within the community. She was a working artist and taught high school art for two years in Houston, Texas, before moving with her husband to Azalea Park in 1978. Her husband moved here to accept a job, and their plan was that he would support her art-making practice until she got on her feet. Their home was on the edge of one of the area's urban canyons, and Pennington quickly came to understand the fire danger posed by improperly managed brush. "I made that transition from artist to activist because of the safety issue. It just seemed like something that I had to do. I didn't do it easily, because I had this great chance to just do my artwork. Anyway, it was the right thing to do."[58] She organized teams of volunteers in her neighborhood to conduct regular brush management and trash cleanups within the miles-long system of snaking canyons that are part of the Chollas Creek watershed that drains into San Diego Bay. She is currently the City Heights community organizer for San Diego Canyonlands,[59] a coalition of "canyon friends" groups that coordinate efforts to clean up, preserve, and restore these ecosystems.

Soon enough, Pennington identified opportunities to integrate art into her activism. She learned to navigate the federal government's Community Development Block Grant Program[60] to enhance her streets with artistic treatments, wrote and received funding from the City of San Diego's Commission for Arts and Culture to restore run-down cultural landmarks, and developed relationships with local and state legislators while lobbying for government support. She describes the challenges of educating herself in such a way: "As an artist, I hated doing the planning, but I see that it's such a valuable piece of what you do. I get it now, but it was hard for me."[61] In addition to preserving the ecosystems, Pennington established an evolving "loop trails" project of creating a contiguous canyon-to-street system of trails and sidewalks that enable hikers to traverse the community. Community art and educational signage are major components in this project. She acknowledges the importance that art and art making has to her personally and in the service of her projects but reflects, "The base of what I was trying to do was safety, cleanup, and that required people getting together. Art grew out of that."[62]

Her skills and experience came in handy in the late 1990s when she got involved in acquiring a piece of vacant land contiguous with a community park and converting it into a water conservation and sculpture garden. For real estate purposes, the land was unbuildable but otherwise privately owned. She worked with then City Councilmember Toni Atkins to procure a grant to purchase the land. Because the city's resources were too limited at the time, the activists agreed to execute a maintenance agreement that requires residents to irrigate the plants and otherwise maintain the space. Pennington reports they schedule work parties once a month. "It takes two people three hours to water. There's some trimming that takes place. I bring barrels, and we've got tools."[63] Neighborhood artists such as Vicki Leon and Jim Bliesner created and installed sculptures in the park. More recent residents in the neighborhood, who do not know the history, experience this garden as simply part of the larger community park.

MANZANITA GATHERING PLACE

The water conservation/sculpture garden became a template for later creating the Manzanita Gathering Place, one of two place-making projects carried out by participants in the Pomegranate Center Fellowship[64] in 2013. The fellowship brought together San Diego artists/community activists, including Pennington, to instruct them in the process of radical community engagement to create place and build social capital. Another participant in the fellowship was Carla Pisbe, Pennington's neighbor and interorganizational collaborator from the Ocean Discovery Institute (ODI),[65] which works on issues of watershed restoration within the canyon system. Because ODI has an established educational relationship with the community's schools, they provided a necessary liaison role for recruiting student volunteers. Pennington remembers:

> I got to know the high school principal and several teachers. Because of those relationships, because Ocean Discovery had their people come in and the principal really promoted it for people to come, we got a really good core group of people to design the thing and participate in the building of it. We pulled together a really good group of people representing the whole community.[66]

Pisbe saw her neighborhood improve as a result of the Manzanita Gathering Place project. She is a native of City Heights and joined the ODI as a ninth-grade student at Hoover High School, which receives the majority of students from the community's middle schools. She joined to learn about science firsthand and through the experience felt empowered to become the first person in her family to go on to college, graduating from University of California Santa Cruz. After graduating in 2011, she returned to accept the environmental stewardship coordinator staff position with ODI, where she oversees watershed education and cleanup efforts in the City Heights urban canyons where she grew up. She has an obvious passion for encouraging local youth in her charge to imagine themselves as college graduates and even eventual scientists as a way of mitigating a condition at her alma mater, where she sees eight hundred entering freshmen, of whom only three hundred enter their senior year and of which just seventy continue on to higher education.[67] She sees her work as an effort to transform traditionally neglected urban canyons into "safe and vibrant environments the community could then enjoy and reclaim as places that are assets."[68]

While attending the Pomegranate Fellowship with Pennington, they advocated for transforming a local blighted vacant lot into what is now the Manzanita Gathering Place. Both Pennington's and Pisbe's groups spread invitations to the neighborhood through word of mouth, flyers, and email lists. Community organizations such as AjA Project, La Maestra, and Price Charities forwarded the invitations to their constituents. Some of these community meetings were held at the art studio of local glass artist Vicki Leon, a few hundred yards from the site. Leon bought her home in Azalea Park over two decades ago, primarily for affordability. After coming to identify with the community, she moved her studio there two and a half years ago and, as a result of connecting to more of the residents, applied for and participated in the Pomegranate Fellowship and helped build the Manzanita Gathering Place.

Through the Manzanita experience, Pisbe saw a canyon overlook in her neighborhood with

> razor wire across the edge and trash everywhere [become a place where] art was able to transform that place and make it look gorgeous and inspire people to really go out there.

[It is now a place where] you see neighbors cleaning up the area, watering those plants, keeping it looking beautiful—it's not turning back in to what it was before.[69]

Just down the hill from the Manzanita Gathering Place, in the urban canyon's watershed, is the future site of ODI's Living Lab that, in addition to becoming their new headquarters, will be a bona fide oceanographic laboratory allowing students from the community to study the relationships between urban runoff and marine life. Designed by local architect Rob Quigley (most famous for San Diego's downtown library, opened in 2013), the lab will incorporate several art pieces and design elements by artists who worked with the architect. It will also serve as staging area and gateway to Pennington's loop trail project. Many of these groups have built strong relations with current City Councilmember Marti Emerald[70] and her staff, who actively participate in canyon cleanups and community gatherings. She is seen as a champion of their community who uses her political acumen to streamline approval of community projects that would otherwise lose steam going through traditional channels.

The Manzanita Gathering Place, as an extension of the Pomegranate Fellowship, was underwritten by the San Diego Foundation, overseen by their director of arts and culture, Felicia Shaw. Shaw previously managed the multimillion dollar Operational Support Program at the City of San Diego's Commission for Arts and Culture for seventeen years. In 2008 she chose to buy a home in Azalea Park because she wanted to participate in the evolution of this neighborhood as not simply an institutional supporter but also a participating resident. After many years of observing the community's work, Shaw chose to buy a home where others also shared the value of creativity and intentionally used it to create a life for themselves.

According to Jim Bliesner, the highest concentrations of existing art in City Heights are along the Fairmount Corridor and further south in his own neighborhood of Azalea Park. In the years since achieving the covered freeway as a conceptual community art piece, he has become an effective educator of community artist/activists, formally teaching urban economic development and design at the UCSD Center for Urban Economics and Design[71] and at Woodbury Architectural School. And he constantly seeks opportunities to bring the brainpower he works with to engage his community, taking "artists out to participate with residents in creating visions."[72] He is currently using that process on a project for the CHCDC to develop a comprehensive art plan for Fairmount Avenue. The study will help develop an understanding of the community's cultural ecology and recommend types of institutional support that will extend and catalyze desirable perceived trends. This process involves enrolling the participation of nonprofits and arts groups in the area, identifying existing walkable destinations as a map for developing artistic and economic enhancements and formulating a long-term, multifaceted funding strategy for identified goals. He worked with AjA Project, located on Fairmount, and spoke to "a group of twenty-one Somali women who are studying photography with them."[73]

Their sharing helped inspire some of the recommended artistic treatments and design elements in his proposal that lean heavily on the tribal and indigenous patterns brought to City Heights by so many immigrants. Although still in proposal phase, Bliesner is confident the work of his students and collaborators will eventually bear fruit. As he notes, half the land in the study area is owned by two property owners, La Maestra and Price Charities, organizations with missions that direct them to serve the existing community's will rather than that of real estate speculators. "The potential for new development is huge; something's going to happen there. They're going to develop their properties."[74]

CONCLUSION

Art is clearly working on many levels in the experiences of City Heights' artists, activists, and community stakeholders. However, the way in which art is working in this community results from a complex and unique set of conditions. Nevertheless, art is impacting civic life in both outcomes as well as a shifting awareness of what is possible when the community works together. It is in recognizing this very uniqueness that an important truth is revealed—each community contains within its already existing ecology a reflection of the public art policy that can best serve it. It would be challenging, to say the least, to craft a regional public art master plan that could effectively address this community's needs while just as effectively addressing the needs of an affluent neighborhood or an area that is designed to serve international tourists. To some extent, art's efficacy in City Heights results from its very history of being underserved. Lower property values here make homeownership considerably more affordable for struggling artists, who, by simply residing in the area, become invested stakeholders that bring their creativity to bear on their shared concerns. Their "artistic concerns" are as much about safety, a clean environment, and community well-being as they are about social theory or the philosophy of aesthetics. In other words, the art is not inserted from outside; it supports the work of already existing activists. As Pennington said, "If we had not been doing the cleanup, I don't think the art would have come. It would have been, like they say, putting lipstick on a pig: you wouldn't do that."[75] And the artists and arts organizations serve as educators and models of how to organize for change in a manner that includes the community at every step. Additionally, the artists do not leave when an art project is complete. They reside in the community, as residents. Their impact is noticed Pisbe acknowledges an improved environment not just in her canyons but also in the built environment. "With AjA you can see them because they are very present on Fairmont Avenue. There are those community places. La Maestra is a very well-used community space; you have Price Charities that if you go into their lobby have all these art displays right in their lobby area."[76] Ainslie sees the value of more traditionally "fine," beautiful, or whimsical art in contexts where such art makes sense. In City Heights, she conceives art's coherency in a particular way. "Public art is about facilitating a dialogue between populations that may not otherwise intersect with one another. It's about building connective tissue and owning space. Because we acknowledge that in order to drive real social progress, you have to engage people in their own change that is internally motivated, not imposed upon them externally."[77]

In conceiving what helpful public art policy would look like in City Heights, two of this study's participants have some thoughts. Bliesner's own recommendation from his Fairmount Avenue cultural asset mapping project suggests we "keep it local. Create a process and have that process certified that allows local artists to do it and participate in it and local decisions for spending it."[78] Ainslie similarly asserts, "Public art should be resident created so that there's ownership over the product."[79] Such a course presents some risk, with less predictable outcomes, if nothing else. But if it's tied to what a community is already doing for itself, one is able to harness kinetic energy rather than hope for potential energy. When questioned about the apparent lack of improved economic indicators after more than a decade of investment, Steve Eldred, who manages the California Endowment's[80] initiative in City Heights said, "It takes a very long time for this approach, but I think it's more sustainable and it's worth the changes you see in the long run. But people have to have patience."[81]

These localized ways of conceiving the value of art and community development in City Heights represents a type of permaculture (permanent culture) thinking, or what Toby Hemenway calls "pattern literacy."[82] Instead of clearing fields, hoeing deep troughs, and planting hybrid seeds to grow a revenue-generating monoculture, permaculturists take the time to simply notice what an ecosystem is already doing well, as with Susholtz's *Mapping the Hood*. Instead of building capital-intensive irrigation systems, they study the watershed and discover where and how moisture is already collecting. Instead of introducing expensive fertilizers into depleted soils, they do the hard work of slowly building the native soil's health, season-by-season. The work of a permaculturalist is to catalyze existing beneficial trend lines, as Bliesner's Fairmount Avenue art study attempts to do in understanding the area's existing cultural ecology. And when one complex system interacts with another complex system, as in the interaction of land-based and marine biology along a coastline, permaculturists look to harness "an intense area of productivity and useful connections."[83] The philosophy of permaculture is not limited by its practitioners to agricultural applications but is expanded as a framework for understanding all complex systems, including human culture, such as those interactions in City Heights. The interaction of health-care systems such as La Maestra with community activism is evolving a self-catalyzing nature, as is the interaction of local groups that work on environmental restoration, fire safety, philanthropy, or education. The various collaborations in the service of shared values energizes and broadens the literacy of the participants. In City Heights, public art does not constitute a distinct system on par with health care or public safety. Rather, it is a signifying practice, a symbolic glue that marshals already existing social practices into a larger aesthetic context that inspires otherwise separate community members to connect through their linked spaces and belong to one another.

NOTES

1. This essay uses Grodach's categorical "community-based" definition of public art; that is, "the production and consumption of art rooted in and reflective of a specific group of people with a shared sense of values and practices based on geographic location and/or identity." Carl Grodach, "Art Spaces in Community and Economic Development: Connections to Neighborhoods, Artists, and the Cultural Economy," *Journal of Planning Education and Research* 31, no.1 (2011): 74.

2. Guetzkow, Joshua, "How the Arts Impact Communities: An Introduction to the Literature on Arts Impact Studies." Paper presented at Taking the Measure of Culture Conference (Princeton University, June 7–8, 2002): 20.

3. Price Charities, "Background," City Heights Initiative website, accessed November 24, 2014, http://cityheightsinitiative.org/background/.

4. SANDAG, *Profile Warehouse*, accessed November 12, 2014, http://profilewarehouse.sandag.org/.

5. Adrian Florido, "A Refugee Hub in City Heights: San Diego Explained," *Voice of San Diego,* September 1, 2011, http://voiceofsandiego.org/2011/09/01/a-refugee-hub-in-city-heights-san-diego-explained/.

6. The IRC is an international relief organization that helps people "whose lives and livelihoods are shattered by conflict and disaster to survive, recover, and gain control of their future" (IRC, "The IRC in San Diego," International Rescue Committee website, accessed October 30, 2014, http://www.rescue.org/us-program/us-san-diego-ca/).

7. Megan Burks, "San Diego's Somali Population: Explained," *Voice of San Diego*, February 22, 2013, http://voiceofsandiego.org/2013/02/22/san-diegos-somali-population-explained/.

8. Price Charities, "Background."

9. Meg Streiff, "Corridors in Chaos: Examining the Consequences of Highway Construction on Urban Communities in San Diego" (master's thesis, San Diego State University, 1994), 63.

10. Ibid, 23.

11. Ibid, 65.

12. IRC, "New Roots Community Farm," International Rescue Committee website, accessed October 30, 2014, http://www.rescue.org/us-program/us-san-diego-ca/fsch/.

13. Installed next to the carrot artwork at the New Roots Community Farm is a sign that reads:

> This artwork commemorates the legacy of The Dancing Carrots which were displayed on the fence of the first community garden in City Heights. The garden was started by neighborhood residents in January 1991 at the site of the SR-15 freeway that now runs through City Heights. For five years prior to the freeway construction the community turned bulldozed land into a beautiful oasis. This design, of a carrot holding a shovel, represents the continuing legacy of community spirit in City Heights.

14. As one community activist recalls that time, "We face inevitable circumstances throughout our lives. Their inevitability doesn't preclude having our hearts broken. Beyond the loss of two city blocks filled with the beauty of a community and their garden was the deep pain of not finding a new home in City Heights" (Anna Daniels, "A Blast from the Past! City Heights Community Garden 1991–1996," *San Diego Free Press,* July 25, 2013, http://sandiegofreepress.org/2012/07/a-blast-from-the-past-city-heights-community-garden-1991-1996/).

15. Community Heights Community Development Corporation, thirty-four years after its founding continues to serve its mission to "enhance the quality of life in City Heights by working with our community to create and sustain quality affordable housing & livable neighborhoods & foster economic self-sufficiency" (CHCDC, "About," CHCDC website, accessed November 24, 2014, http://www.cityheightscdc.org/about/).

16. Jim Bliesner, interview by Nigel Brookes, October 1, 2014, interview 8, transcript.

17. Ibid.

18. Anna Daniels, "A Freeway Runs through It: A City Heights-Barrio Logan Conversation," *San Diego Free Press*, April 24, 2013, http://sandiegofreepress.org/2013/04/a-freeway-runs-through-it-a-city-heights-barrio-logan-conversation/.

19. Jim Bliesner, interview.

20. City of San Diego Commission for Arts and Culture, Call for Artists: Documenting San Diego's City Heights Community, released May 19, 2009, City of San Diego Commission for Arts and Culture, Public Art Program.

21. Ibid.

22. Founded in 2000, AjA Project is an acronym for the phrase "Autosuficiencia Juntada con Apoyo," which loosely translates as "supporting self-sufficiency." Their mission is to provide photography-based programming to transform the lives of youth and communities. Their headquarters are located on Fairmount Avenue, across the street from La Maestra Community Clinic. AjA Project, "Ways Participatory Photography Impacts Youth," AjA Project website, accessed November 20, 2014, http://www.ajaproject.org/html/method.html/.

23. Lynn Susholtz, interview by Nigel Brookes, September 29, 2014, interview 1, transcript.

24. Ibid.

25. Ibid.

26. The San Diego Foundation is a self-defined community foundation with a mission to "improve the quality of life in all San Diego communities by providing leadership for effective philanthropy that builds enduring assets and by promoting community solutions through research, convenings and actions that advance the common good." http://www.sdfoundation.org/AboutUs/Mission,Vision,Values.aspx

27. Lynn Susholtz, interview.

28. Ibid.

29. Art Produce is Lynn Susholtz's art studio and gallery, behind which she has created an outdoor urban garden and performance space. Located approximately one mile from La Maestra Health Center, she utilizes her space as a location for "integrating community voice and vision into the cultural and physical landscape through art and education" (Lynn Susholtz, Art Produce website, accessed November 20, 2014, http://www.artproduce.org/).

30. Lynn Susholtz, interview.

31. Ibid.

32. Ibid.

33. La Maestra Community Health Centers began in 1990 to provide new citizens with not just basic medical care but also housing, employment, and other services that would support their needs. Their mission is "to provide quality healthcare and education, improve the overall well-being of the family, bringing the underserved, ethnically diverse communities into the mainstream of our society, through a caring, effective, culturally- and linguistically competent manner, respecting the dignity of all patients" (La Maestra, "History and Mission," La Maestra website, accessed December 20, 2014, http://www.lamaestra.org/history-and-mission/default.html/).

34. Initiated in 2010, La Maestra's CHA program includes both temporary exhibits and a permanent collection of art by emerging and established local artists, representing a broad range of media, styles, and cultures; opportunities for artists-in-residence; a retail gallery; and performing arts presentations in the City Heights health center. CHA is designed to integrate quality art experiences into the lives of everyone who visits La Maestra; invigorate the identity, pride, and vitality of City Heights; and contribute to healing and acculturation processes for residents.

35. Lynn Susholtz, interview.

36. Zara Marselian, interview by Nigel Brookes, October 2, 2014, interview 9, transcript.

37. Ibid.

38. Ibid.

39. Ibid.

40. Ibid.

41. Ibid.

42. Ibid.

43. In 2005, Price Charities purchased property on the northwest intersection of Fairmount and University avenues to be built in four phases, which included affordable housing for seniors, a mixed-use commercial facility, the 30,000-square-foot La Maestra Health Center, and the 5,400-square-foot City Heights Square Mini Community Park.

44. Matthew Hervey, interview by Nigel Brookes, September 17, 2014, interview 4, transcript.

45. Ibid.

46. Megan Burks, "San Diego's Richest Poor Neighborhood, Two Decades Later," *KPBS Public Broadcasting,* November 18, 2014, http://www.kpbs.org/news/2014/nov/18/san-diegos-richest-poor-neighborhood-two-decades-l/.

47. Wendell Kling, interview by Nigel Brookes, November 5, 2014, interview 15, transcript.

48. "Permaculture" is a term used to describe an evolving set of agricultural and human cultural practices that are designed for sustainability and resiliency. It is defined by one practitioner as "a conscious design system for creating sustainable human habitats that are deeply rooted in the unique characteristics of the place" (Seth Mozerkatz and Justin Ritchie, "Permaculture Convergence," Notes from Extraenvironmentalist Podcast 57, podcast audio, July 4, 2012, http://www.extraenvironmentalist.com/2013/07/04/permaculture-convergence-jenny-pell-edible-forest-gardening/).

49. Wendell Kling, interview.

50. OSP is the Organizational Support Program, an annual operating funding program managed by the City of San Diego Commission for Arts and Culture. The OSP and the project-specific Creative Communities San Diego (CCSD) support over 120 organizations throughout San Diego each year. In addition to the Kling and Susholtz artworks managed through the commission's public art program, these funding programs support a Vietnamese Lantern Festival, dance troupes, a puppet guild, street fairs, community parades, and artists-in-schools in City Heights each year. This foundation of support helps stabilize organizations involved in cultural production in this community.

51. Sandra Ainslie, interview by Nigel Brookes, September 5, 2014, interview 6, transcript.

52. Ibid.

53. Ibid.

54. Ibid.

55. Ibid.

56. Ibid.

57. Ibid.

58. Linda Pennington, interview by Nigel Brookes, September 17, 2014, interview 7, transcript.

59. San Diego Canyonlands' mission is "to promote, protect and restore the natural habitats in San Diego County canyons and creeks by fostering education and ongoing community involvement in stewardship and advocacy, and by collaborating with other organizations." http://sdcanyonlands.org/about-us/mission-vision-and-values

60. The Community Development Block Grant (CDBG), one of the longest-running programs of the U.S. Department of Housing and Urban Development, funds local community development activities such as affordable housing, antipoverty programs, and infrastructure development. CDBGs, like other block grant programs, differ from categorical grants, made for specific purposes, in that they are subject to less federal oversight and are largely used at the discretion of the state and local governments and their subgrantees. "Community Development Block Grant," http://portal.hud.gov/hudportal/HUD?src=/program_offices/comm_planning/communitydevelopment/programs

61. Linda Pennington, interview.

62. Ibid.

63. Ibid.

64. For over twenty-seven years, the Washington State–based Pomegranate Center has been creating art-based gathering places as a location for generating social capital. In 2013 the San Diego Foundation sponsored a four-month-long fellowship training that included hands on experience in community organizing, design, and construction and art fabrication/installation. The fellowship resulted in two completed projects, the second of which is Manzanita Gathering Place in City Heights (Pomegranate Center website, accessed November 19, 2014, http://pomegranatecenter.org/).

65. ODI was created ten years ago to leverage San Diego's natural environments as a means to engage young people from underserved communities and inspire them to become part of the next generation of scientific and environmental leaders ("Why an Ocean Discovery Institute?" Ocean Discovery Institute website, accessed November 24, 2014, http://oceandiscoveryinstitute.org/about-us/purpose/).

66. Linda Pennington, interview.

67. The statistics referenced by Pisbe were extrapolated from three pages in the California Postsecondary Education Commission website: California Postsecondary Education Commission, "Detailed Data," accessed January 19, 2015, http://www.cpec.ca.gov/OnlineData/HSCollegeDestEthnicity.asp?CDSCode=37683383732997&Year=2008/; http://www.cpec.ca.gov/OnLineData/HSOutreach.asp?CDSCode=37683383732997/; and http://www.cpec.ca.gov/onlinedata/FreshmenPathwayChart.asp?Inst=373299.

68. Carla Pisbe, interview by Nigel Brookes, October 3, 2014, interview 10, transcript.

69. Ibid.

70. Marti Emerald is the City of San Diego councilmember for District 9, which contains City Heights. Prior to being elected to office in 2008, she was a television journalist for thirty years, primarily as a consumer advocate. Her explicit political support for arts in City Heights is informed by a long-term cultural literacy, growing up as a self-described "song-and-dance kid" who performed in theater from middle school through college. From her experience as a councilmember, she has observed art in City Heights effectively "connecting people and bringing communities together" ("Councilmember Marti Emerald, Council District 9," City of San Diego website, accessed November 10, 2014, http://www.sandiego.gov/citycouncil/cd9/).

71. Jim Bliesner is one of two directors of the Center for Urban Economics and Design, a nonprofit organization working in partnership with the University of California, San Diego, and Woodbury Architectural School to bridge the gaps between academic disciplines, business, community, and public policy in an effort to address strategic urban issues on a local, regional, state, and national level, all by utilizing a multidisciplinary approach that aims to create a synergistic convergence of urban design and economic sustainability (CUED, "Mission Statement," Center for Urban Economics and Design website, accessed November 16, 2014, http://cued-ucsd.org/aboutmission.php?id=1/).

72. Jim Bliesner, interview.

73. Ibid.

74. Ibid.

75. Linda Pennington, interview.

76. Carla Pisbe, interview.

77. Sandra Ainslie, interview.

78. Jim Bliesner, interview.

79. Sandra Ainslie, interview.

80. Founded in 1996, the California Endowment is a private, California-focused health foundation that advocates for health and health equity and raises awareness of how and where health can happen. The endowment does this by working to expand access to affordable, quality care for underserved communities and investing in fundamental improvements for the health of all Californians. In 2010 the California Endowment embarked on an interorganizational ten-year effort to improve health in City Heights. A requirement of this initiative is that any new infrastructure created for the community must be because residents felt empowered, demanded it, and were heard by elected officials.

81. Megan Burks, "San Diego's Richest Poor Neighborhood."

82. Toby Hemenway, "What Permaculture Isn't—and Is." *Pattern Literacy*, accessed November 24, 2014, http://www.patternliteracy.com/668-what-permaculture-isnt-and-is/.

83. "Permaculture," *Wikipedia*, accessed December 15, 2014, https://en.wikipedia.org/wiki/Permaculture

REFERENCES

Ainslie, Sandra. Interview 6 by Nigel Brookes. September 5, 2014.

AjA Project. "Ways Participatory Photography Impacts Youth." AjA Project website. Accessed November 20, 2014. http://www.ajaproject.org/html/method.html.

Bliesner, Jim. Interview 8 by Nigel Brookes. October 1, 2014.

———. "I-15 in City Heights: How a Freeway That Divided the Community Became an Urban Monument to Citizen Activism." *San Diego Free Press.* August 22, 2013. http://sandiegofreepress.org/2013/08/i-15-in-city-heights-how-a-freeway-that-divided-the-community-became-an-urban-monument-to-citizen-activism/#.VFZ%E2%80%A6/.

Burks, Megan. "San Diego's Richest Poor Neighborhood, Two Decades Later." *KPBS Public Broadcasting.* November 18, 2014. http://www.kpbs.org/news/2014/nov/18/san-diegos-richest-poor-neighborhood-two-decades-l/.

———. "San Diego's Somali Population: Explained." *Voice of San Diego.* February 22, 2013. http://voiceofsandiego.org/2013/02/22/san-diegos-somali-population-explained/.

California Postsecondary Education Commission. *Detailed Data.* Accessed January 19, 2015. http://www.cpec.ca.gov/SecondPages/DetailedData.asp/.

CHCDC. "About Us." Community Heights Community Development Corporation website. Accessed November 24, 2014. http://www.cityheightscdc.org/about/.

City of San Diego Commission for Arts and Culture. Call for Artists: Documenting San Diego's City Heights Community. Released May 19, 2009. City of San Diego Commission for Arts and Culture, Public Art Program.

"Community Development Block Grant." http://portal.hud.gov/hudportal/HUD?src=/pro gram_offices/comm_planning/communitydevelopment/programs

"Councilmember Marti Emerald, Council District 9." City of San Diego website. http://www .sandiego.gov/citycouncil/cd9/.

CUED. "Mission Statement." Center for Urban Economics and Design website. Accessed November 16, 2014. http://cued-ucsd.org/aboutmission.php?id=1/.

Daniels, Anna. "A Blast from the Past! City Heights Community Garden 1991–1996." *San Diego Free Press.* July 25, 2013. http://sandiegofreepress.org/2012/07/a-blast-from-the -past-city-heights-community-garden-1991-1996/.

———. "A Freeway Runs Through It: A City Heights-Barrio Logan Conversation." *San Diego Free Press.* April 24, 2013. http://sandiegofreepress.org/2013/04/a-freeway-runs-through-it- a-city-heights-barrio-logan-conversation/.

Florido, Adrian. "A Refugee Hub in City Heights: San Diego Explained." *Voice of San Diego.* September 1, 2011. http://voiceofsandiego.org/2011/09/01/a-refugee-hub-in-city-heights -san-diego-explained/.

Grodach, Carl. "Art Spaces in Community and Economic Development: Connections to Neighborhoods, Artists, and the Cultural Economy." *Journal of Planning Education and Research* 31, no. 1 (2011): 74–85.

Guetzkow, Joshua. "How the Arts Impact Communities: An Introduction to the Literature on Arts Impact Studies." Paper presented at Taking the Measure of Culture Conference. Princeton University, June 7–8, 2002.

Hervey, Matthew. Interview 4 by Nigel Brookes. September 17, 2014.

Hemenway, Toby. "What Permaculture Isn't—and Is." *Pattern Literacy.* Accessed November 24, 2014. http://www.patternliteracy.com/668-what-permaculture-isnt-and-is/.

IRC. "The IRC in San Diego." International Rescue Committee website. Accessed October 30, 2014. http://www.rescue.org/us-program/us-san-diego-ca.

———. "New Roots Community Farm." International Rescue Committee website. Accessed October 30, 2014. http://www.rescue.org/us-program/us-san-diego-ca/fsch.

Kling, Wendell. Interview 15 by Nigel Brookes. November 5, 2014.

La Maestra. "History and Mission." La Maestra website. Accessed December 20, 2014. http:// www.lamaestra.org/history-and-mission/default.html.

Marselian, Zara. Interview 9 by Nigel Brookes. October 2, 2014.

Mozerkatz, Seth, and Justin Ritchie. "Permaculture Convergence." Notes from Extraenvi- ronmentalist Podcast 57. Podcast audio. July 4, 2012. http://www.extraenvironmentalist .com/2013/07/04/permaculture-convergence-jenny-pell-edible-forest-gardening/.

Ocean Discovery Institute. "Why an Ocean Discovery Institute?" Ocean Discovery Institute website. Accessed November 24, 2014. http://oceandiscoveryinstitute.org/about-us/purpose/.

Pennington, Linda. Interview 7 by Nigel Brookes. September 17, 2014.

"Permaculture." *Wikipedia.* Accessed December 15, 2014. https://en.wikipedia.org/wiki/ Permaculture

Pisbe, Carla. Interview 10 by Nigel Brookes. October 3, 2014.

Pomegranate Center website. Accessed November 19, 2014. http://pomegranatecenter.org/.

Price Charities. "Background." City Heights Initiative website. Accessed November 24, 2014. http://cityheightsinitiative.org/background/.

SANDAG (San Diego Association of Governments). *Profile Warehouse.* Accessed November 12, 2014. http://profilewarehouse.sandag.org/.

Streiff, Meg. "Corridors in Chaos: Examining the Consequences of Highway Construction on Urban Communities in San Diego." Master's thesis, San Diego State University, 1994.

Susholtz, Lynn. Art Produce website. Accessed November 20, 2014. http://www.artproduce.org/.

———. Interview 1 by Nigel Brookes. September 29, 2014.

10

Secrets of a Public Art Administrator

How to Help Your City Thrive through the Magic of Public Art

Felicia Filer

> Civic engagement means working to make a difference in the civic life of our communities and developing the combination of knowledge, skills, values and motivation to make that difference. It means promoting the quality of life in a community, through both political and nonpolitical processes.
>
> —Thomas Ehrlich[1]

INTRODUCTION

This chapter describes ways in which the Los Angeles Department of Cultural Affairs (DCA) maximizes the value of public art through the strategic orchestration of its public art process to create civic engagement that unfolds over time. In our city, we have over many years developed techniques for leveraging public art to improve the quality of life for Angelinos in ways that go far beyond the impact of the artwork itself in relation to its audience.

We owe our effectiveness, we believe, to the specific ways in which our department relates to two considerations—first, stakeholder dynamics in civic engagement; and second, the potential outcomes that can be achieved through public art. Over the past two decades, our knowledge of these two areas has grown to encompass concepts that we have not seen acknowledged in the public discourse in the field. This chapter enlarges the discourse of what public art ideally can achieve and expands the understanding of potential outcomes of civic engagement.

COURTING POTENTIAL STAKEHOLDERS: A FLUID PROCESS

Most often, public art programs view civic engagement as the public response to a work of art after it has been installed and unveiled to the community. Or it is seen as the amount of outreach needed to elicit an acceptable turnout at a community meeting early in the artwork's development. Yet we believe that these perspectives are too narrow and present a static view of civic engagement. At DCA we have learned that civic engagement is anything but static—it is a fluid process, and the focus can fluctuate between internal city departments and external community stakeholders over the life of a project. The three projects described in the following pages exemplify this dynamic and illustrate our strategies to maximize engagement: in particular, by widening the perception of potential stakeholders to include city staff, we engage them as we would public stakeholders, addressing their concerns and serving their interests, thereby building goodwill and attracting additional resources. The projects also show the benefits that accrue from public art processes that are informed by a nuanced concept of civic engagement as a fluid interplay between internal and external stakeholders.

PICKING YOUR TARGETS: AN EXPANDED ARRAY OF PUBLIC ART BENEFITS

Because the full range of benefits that public art can achieve is not generally articulated, we bring the following enumeration to the public discourse to encourage public art administrators to aim high, establishing targets for achievement that go beyond the expected public art outcomes.

The public art process can create civic engagement of two general categories: (1) civic engagement centered around the art itself—that is, engagement with the artwork and the artist, including arts participation and audience engagement—and (2) civic engagement relating to general issues of public concern. These categories are not mutually exclusive; in fact, many, if not most, outcomes of any given project can be applied to both of them. Yet this distinction is useful for tracking the impact of artworks to show how they enhance the community's overall quality of life. At DCA we leverage the public art process to create maximal engagement in both categories, leading to the greatest number of benefits to the community. As the department has developed new approaches, we have seen—to our surprise and delight—a continual expansion in our understanding of the wide-ranging possible impacts of public art projects.

BENEFITS OF ENGAGEMENT WITH THE ART ITSELF

> Creativity is a continuity that engenders itself in others. . . . Art is not art, therefore, except as it leads to an engendering creativity in its beholders.
>
> —James Carse, *Finite and Infinite Games*

First, the artwork is the heart of the public art project. The primary benefits derived from the audience encounter with the artwork are, of course, the aesthetic experience, perhaps including joy and pleasure, as well as the intellectual interest stimulated by the artwork. There may be an educational component too, as individuals learn that art can be fun and outrageous or intimate and accessible on a human scale. Presentations by artists who address community members as respected peers are also educational. And the artwork itself can inspire creativity among its audience as well as stimulate the programming of future art events in the venue where the public art is located.

When a permanent public artwork is installed in a public building, it has the effect of energizing the facility, transforming it into a new cultural space that has the power to catalyze future artistic production in the same space. An example of this dynamic is the Van Nuys FlyAway bus terminal, discussed later, where the transportation hub, transformed into a cultural space by a permanent public artwork installed at the entrance, has inspired an ongoing series of new performances over the last four years.

BENEFITS OF ENGAGEMENT
ADDRESSING GENERAL PUBLIC CONCERNS

Second, we come to the benefits derived from civic engagement designed to address general issues of public concern. There are positive economic impacts, including mitigation of neighborhood blight; the gentrification that comes with new businesses attracted by the improved area, such as coffeehouses and art galleries; and the commercial value that accrues when the artwork raises the profile of the venue, building its capacity to market itself and its services—developments that could result in new jobs. The creation of the artwork itself supports small businesses (fabricators, installers, structural engineers, lighting designers, and so on), and the development of artists' skill sets builds their capacity to thrive. Moreover, DCA continually provides technical support to artists and arts organizations, guiding them in the process of working in the public realm.

Important social and political benefits are derived from the partnerships that are formed among community members during the public art process, the building of goodwill between citizens and government, and the development of a self-identified and engaged stakeholder community. The public art process can be a spectacular tool for uncovering points of tension in the community, leading to solutions that resolve those tensions or provide other quality-of-life enhancements. These might include the reshaping of public attitudes and subsequent actions, such as the engagement of lower socioeconomic communities through exposure to contemporary public art, which results in the promotion of social equity and justice as lower-income neighborhoods are given equal access to public art resources. Finally, the visibility of diversity in race and gender among public artists—and sometimes embodied in artistic images themselves—serves to counter cultural stereotyping and affirm the contributions and creativity of all our residents.

The projects discussed in this chapter, especially the Sixth Street Bridge and the Traffic Islands Gateway, illustrate public benefits in many arenas that contribute to the quality of life in Los Angeles.

The First Hurdle: Overcoming Staff Resistance

Historically, before we could begin to engage the public, we had a major hurdle to overcome: the resistance of city staff. While we have made great progress in this area over almost two decades, resistance remains a central concern of our public art strategy. Often the interaction between city departments is the place where the value and role of the art component in the overall project are determined. In the past, the artwork was commonly met with resistance, if not resentment. Even today, the project team, usually composed of engineers, architects, and finance staff, is likely to have predetermined ideas about what the public artwork should be—namely, a decorative and stand-alone object. It is also generally assumed that the public artwork will have minimal bearing on the larger civic issues at stake and that, therefore, its realization should take place late in a project's development. Public art is typically seen as the icing on the cake, so to speak. In effect, this attitude marginalizes the public artwork and the process that leads to it and robs the art component of its ability to generate valuable civic engagement from the beginning of the project.

In 1996, when I joined DCA, the project engineers and architects implementing city capital improvement projects used many tactics to evade the public art program. Their wiles would include requesting that their project be exempt from the public art requirement or stealthily underrepresenting the art budget by not calculating the full 1 percent. Or they might not bring a project to our attention until it was at 100 percent design, when opportunities for the artwork itself, as well as for creating civic engagement, are minimal. Architects would attempt to relegate the artwork to a pedestal in an out-of-the-way location or reserve a wall clear for a "mural" to be located in an inconspicuous place where it would not interfere with the building. Such willful subversion by city engineers and architects left the public art completely on its own. The resistance between the staff of other city departments and Cultural Affairs was expressed in such admonitions as "Stay out of our way"; "You are on your own to complete 'your' project"; and "Make sure you don't disrupt the construction schedule, because if you do, we will blame the public art for any delays."

Over the years, we have found effective ways to mitigate and even transform the entrenched resistance of city staff. The first thing we did was to develop internal project management guidelines and systems to ensure that every public art project was completed on time. Once they saw that the art schedule could keep up with the building schedule, project engineers began to trust both our department and the artists, and they would relax about the public art. We also developed specific language for project managers to include in architects' contracts and general contractors' bid documents; it presents the requirements for interacting with and providing assistance to the artist. And to ensure that we can pay for any unforeseen change orders associated with the installation, we withhold a percentage of the public art budget. Finally, we assign the risk of determining when the artist can proceed with fabrication to the project manager, to assure a "just in time" delivery for the artwork. Through such steps we have made significant headway in overcoming the resistance of city staff. These approaches create the relationships and attitudes that support the successful completion of a project, which ends, but only nominally, in the installation of the artwork.

CREATING A NEW CULTURAL SPACE: VAN NUYS FLYAWAY DANCE PROJECT BY SARAH ELGART

This bus terminal, located in the San Fernando Valley, offers transportation to Los Angeles International Airport (LAX), thereby relieving congestion on the freeways and at the airport. The community is devoid of cultural amenities except for a prominent public artwork at the terminal's entrance, installed in 2009. In 2010, alarmed by low ridership, the bus terminal management asked for our help. Our response was to utilize the existing public artwork—a tangible marker of culture in the area—as a lever to stimulate new cultural activity in the terminal. We commissioned a series of site-specific dance performances to offer the community fresh and dynamic cultural experiences as well as to market the bus service. The performance program did indeed convert the bus terminal into a popular cultural space for the community and was instrumental in building clientele for the airport bus service.

I got the idea for a dance performance from a delightful event generated in 2009 by one of our public artists, Stephen Glassman. One day, about a year before the FlyAway sent out their SOS, I attended the unveiling of his new public artwork, a large sculpture in a public plaza at the entrance to a private office building. Glassman had commissioned his wife, dancer and choreographer Sarah Elgart of Arrogant Elbow, to create a site-specific performance emphasizing the normal path of travel through the space by drawing the audience from the parking lot, through the plaza, around the sculpture, and into the building.

Through this interactive performance, Glassman brought the sculpture to life with movement and music. I saw that by introducing performances or other arts programming into locations where we had already installed permanent artworks, we could activate and enliven those spaces, changing the perception and use of the space while adding a new dimension to the original artwork. Thus Elgart's creativity, building on Glassman's, inspired the idea that at such sites, DCA could commission creative artworks that would offer substantial value—through audience engagement with the art itself as well as from the public art project's contribution to matters of general public concern.

In 2010 we sat down with Elgart to discuss the idea of creating a site-specific performance for the Van Nuys FlyAway. The terminal is in an industrial area that adjoins low-income apartments. In addition to the lack of cultural amenities, the neighborhood was neither pedestrian nor bicycle friendly, and there were no open green spaces. Our challenge was to create civic engagement in the form of a dialogue or activity—in a community where there was none.

We decided to use dance to amplify the concepts of "movement" and "transportation" inherent in bus travel, and our plan was for Arrogant Elbow to perform in several indoor and outdoor spaces. We allocated a budget of $15,800, and LAX management, which oversees the bus service, approved a site-specific dance program. Yet the FlyAway's staff was hesitant about the dance project; the facility's manager, citing potential liability, declared pretty much every space "off limits" to the choreographer. So it happened that the dancers could use only a few areas inside the terminal.

But then something happened: the bus terminal staff, viewing rehearsals for the work, *Fly Away Home*, witnessed the process of how a dance composition develops, and they saw Elgart safely utilizing the space. Travelers to and from LAX became fascinated as they watched the choreography unfold. One of them didn't want to board his bus; he wished he could stay and watch the dancers. The staff began to relax and identify with the piece—it was theirs now. They offered Elgart more territory and spontaneously started directing passengers away from the performers, protecting *their* dancers from the terminal's clients. Elgart devised a dance sequence that took place around employees' workstations so that they became incorporated into the piece. Gradually the boundary between dancers and staff softened and then dissolved. There was a mood of exhilaration when FlyAway personnel began to adopt the view that *they themselves* were creative, as they experienced the "choreography" of their own body language incorporated into the stream of the professional dancers' movements.

On the night of the performance, July 2, 2011, the FlyAway terminal was filled with over two hundred spectators who had come out to see the performance, thanks to Arrogant Elbow's intensive publicity. As travelers returning from LAX disembarked with their luggage, the dancers joined the parade of passengers and created a playful melding of dancers, passengers, staff, and audience. By the end of the performance, the attitudes of the terminal's staff and management had been transformed.

Many audience members, despite the fact that they lived in the area, hadn't known about the FlyAway. When LAX management realized that dance performances could be an excellent marketing tool, they asked us to continue programming events there.

Here the civic engagement strategy bridged a number of objectives. The bus terminal is now a nontraditional performing arts space in this underserved and culturally desolated area. Since Elgart's spectacular inaugural dance, our ongoing programming of performances continues to build awareness and increase use of the FlyAway service. Because the venue's proximity to apartments makes it easy for local residents to walk over and see an event, the dance series has created pedestrian-friendly opportunities for the community, in addition to offering the intrinsic value of enjoyable and enlivening dance performances.

UNITING COMPETING COMMUNITIES:
TRAFFIC ISLANDS GATEWAY PROJECT BY KIM ABELES

This project—linking two traffic islands in South Los Angeles—demonstrates the use of public art as an intervention to promote harmony between two neighborhoods with competing needs and contested resources. One community group wanted more open, green space and had, in fact, won a lawsuit whose court-mandated settlement obligated the city to provide a green-space amenity in a large traffic island located at Jefferson Boulevard and Rodeo Road. This first group envisioned lush green trees and landscaping, with attractive benches for seating. Simultaneously, a group from an adjacent community wanted a tall, presumably bronze statue of Martin Luther King Jr. in another, smaller traffic island at the intersection of Martin Luther King Jr. Boulevard and Rodeo Road.

DCA learned about the plans for the large traffic island in 2011 when we were contacted by Gus Malkoun of the Bureau of Engineering (BOE), project manager for an air treatment facility. We scheduled a meeting with the BOE team, local city council office representatives, and community members, where some of the attendees, from a second, adjacent community with an undeveloped traffic island, spoke up about their desire for public art. Together DCA and BOE approached the city council district office, obtained funding for the second project, and then combined it with the air treatment facility funds to create a budget of $150,000 for a single artwork to be situated at both sites. Using information gleaned from the meeting, we created a vision statement and issued a request for proposals.

Our conceptual approach was to treat the islands, both conceptually and visually, as a pair and to style them as "gateways" to the two communities. The challenge for artist Kim Abeles was to transform these barren traffic islands into a single artwork that addressed the wishes of both communities. The work—based on the theme "Walk a mile in my shoes"—includes images of the shoes of people who marched with King and of activists who have contributed to our city. While there is no tall bronze statue, the small island contains a memorial to King and other national heroes of the civil rights movement, and the large island focuses on local community activists. The traffic islands are located precisely one mile apart, and the artwork invites members of the two communities to "walk in one another's shoes," exchanging places as they literally walk a mile and bring the metaphor of the work's title to life.

BOE's concerns related strictly to the budget and the schedule. Malkoun, who had little experience with public art, warned us repeatedly that the artist needed to "deliver the project within the budget and deliver it on time," while making it clear that he had no confidence this would happen. To allay his fears, we increased the frequency of communications and meetings and brought him into the art-making process much more intimately than is usual; we even invited him to Abeles's studio and to her fabricators' workplaces. DCA also proactively managed Abeles's time table to enable her to get ahead of the overall project schedule.

The artist completed her project within budget and on time in June 2014. Throughout the project, Malkoun's resistant and suspicious attitude toward the public art and artist was slowly transformed into advocacy and gratitude, and he is now an enthusiastic convert to public art. In 2014 he entered the public art–enhanced project into a competition and was honored with an award by the American Public Works Association. Now Malkoun advocates that the artwork educates, inspires, and generates a sense of pride.

The project did indeed defuse the competition for resources and demonstrably united the two communities—an outcome achieved through the civic engagement created during the steps of the public art process. These steps included outreach to both communities to identify local heroes and capture their stories for inclusion in the art project; work with a local poet, Beverly Lafontaine, to create a poem specifically for this project; and the artist's development of a website detailing the accomplishments of the individuals honored in the piece. And then, of course, there was the civic engagement created through the final artwork itself. The work created two outdoor cultural spaces that will attract future arts activities as well.

STRATEGIC ORCHESTRATION OF THE PROCESS: SIXTH STREET BRIDGE PROJECT BY GLENN KAINO

The Sixth Street Viaduct ("Bridge") public art project epitomizes the classic *West Side Story* archetype. A historic bridge must be torn down to make way for a new bridge, and the communities flanking the bridge—one affluent and gentrified, the other working class—have different needs and issues. Artist Glenn Kaino is in the process of developing a social engagement and community participation strategy that will inform the design of the public artwork, scheduled to be installed in 2019. Moreover, one of the design principles is that the artwork must serve as an open-ended infrastructure that allows for other artists to create projects on and around it.

In 2012 the DCA received a call from project manager John Chu of the BOE. Chu had worked with us on twenty other bridge projects, so he was a convert to public art. He wanted to tell us about a large infrastructure project he was working on that would have a substantial public art investment. We were contacted at the project's conception—a rarity. We set up a meeting with Chu and the project's chief administrative officer. Chu wanted to discuss the "tight" budget. He also wanted to know how long it would take to select an artist. Not so fast!

We asked for any information (council instructions, internal reports, meeting notes, PowerPoint presentations) that would help us get up to speed. The BOE had established a significant civic engagement component, including a project website, newsletter, and content for social media platforms—more than we had ever seen. We were excited, realizing that the public art process could contribute to the overall project solution because it would be integrated at the onset. We told Chu that we would go over the project's total budget with him later, once it was finalized, to make sure the full 1 percent for art was calculated. Curiously, the budget figure he had named was significantly lower than the mandated 1 percent of total construction costs.

The following week, we met with the engineering team. A structurally degenerating iconic bridge traversing the Los Angeles River in the middle of the city was to be demolished, and the city would build a new, mile-long bridge spanning the working-class community of Boyle Heights on the east and the trendy industrial Arts District on the west. This was going to be a massive undertaking.

Soon five architectural firms, selected through an international competition, presented conceptual designs to the public. In keeping with our general strategy to attend every meeting we can, both internal and external, and to listen intently for community input, we saw each presentation, focusing on comments from the audience.

As we continued to go to project meetings, it became clear that there were many unresolved community issues inherent in the bridge project. On the east, there is a large working-class Latino population in Boyle Heights, a neighborhood with a long history of murals and home to most of the city's historically significant murals. While Boyle Heights has a vibrant cultural life, its arts and cultural institutions, with scant resources, are underdeveloped. The arts community was tightly focused on art production—specifically, how could the project's public art dollars pay local muralists to paint new murals in the vicinity of the bridge?

The west side of the bridge is located in downtown Los Angeles. Primarily white, affluent professionals have gentrified the area, which is replete with endowed cultural institutions; costly and architecturally distinguished buildings; high-end restaurants, coffee shops and breweries; art galleries, art walks, artists' studios; and so on. This contingent wanted public art monies to be used for performance or other cultural events that they could "consume."

During the meetings, community members from both sides of the bridge spoke of their longstanding concerns, frustrations, needs, and desires, many of which had not been addressed by the city for years. As we listened, we paid particular attention to any hints of unmet cultural needs in the two neighborhoods, for these were issues that would have to be one of the central matters addressed by the public art. The beauty was that by satisfying these interests, many issues of general concern would also be addressed, such as promoting the visibility of economic redress between the two communities.

The community wanted an active role in the project development, so to keep the public informed, BOE developed the website, newsletter, and social media content mentioned previously. Additionally, BOE formed the volunteer Design Aesthetic Advisory Committee, composed of community members and design professionals, to provide guidance during architectural development. With this in mind, we formulated a parallel strategy and created the Public Art Advisory Committee (PAAC), consisting of community arts stakeholders, to provide outside input and review and minimize internal and external resistance. This approach would also contribute to integrating the overall project cohesively so that the art would not be perceived—by the bridge team or the public—as a separate entity. Thus we elevated the public art to the same playing field as that of the entire project by using the same channels of community outreach, by developing a similar process for civic engagement, and by adopting the same vocabulary.

Next we arranged for the architectural team to present the bridge design to the PAAC. This was a powerful gesture to the committee members, because it signaled that their participation was so important that it warranted an exclusive presentation by the team. Then the committee visited the bridge and experienced crossing it together. As a result of this "field trip" and mindful of the symbolic impact, they agreed to hold a brainstorming meeting at an art gallery in Boyle Heights rather than in downtown Los Angeles. Ultimately, the committee arrived at the following vision for the public art: to be open-ended and a place for additional creative activities to occur in the future. Thus, for the first time, the public art component was acknowledged in the written goals of a public art project for its potential to be the catalyst and location of future cultural production.

The project engineering team did not know quite what to think of this vision statement. But we had their attention. Now it seemed that the project team wanted the public art component to function as a full partner on the project, not just an add-on. The art budget was established at the full 1 percent value, $1.2 million. At the next community meeting, with PAAC members in the audience, our staff presented the PAAC's work, including the vision statement for the public art. We also introduced committee members, showing the community that these people were their neighbors.

Next we formed the standard five-member Artist Selection Committee (ASC), made up of working artists, university art professors, and contemporary art curators. Forgoing a request for qualifications because of time constraints, we asked each of them to nominate four artists, and the five highest-scoring artists were interviewed. Los Angeles artist Glenn Kaino was selected based on his connection to Boyle Heights and downtown Los Angeles, on his understanding of the politics of the bridge, and, most important, on his facility with technology and his enthusiasm for incorporating social media into the public art process. One month later, in April 2014, the city council district office held a press event on the bridge to introduce him to the community.

CONCLUSION

The three projects discussed in this chapter demonstrate strategies DCA used to overcome the resistance of city staff, resolve tensions effectively, and accomplish specific civic outcomes. The artworks bring the public new aesthetic experiences that can be beautiful, inspiring, fun, and educational. In addition, these public art projects provided innovative solutions tailored to particular social problems that had been identified, and they established new public gathering and cultural spaces.

This is important because today there is a growing demand in cities for more public gathering spaces, and in the gathering spaces, as we have observed in Los Angeles, people want to have artistic experiences. These new activities, which broaden the perception of what is traditionally thought of as public art, can then be rolled over into new civic engagement, particularly civic engagement centered around the art itself. In the new cultural spaces, the public can decide what types of art or cultural projects are produced there, and those in turn invite more civic participation to program the spaces over time.

In Los Angeles, our view of the concept of civic engagement, as part of the public art process, includes internal city departments as stakeholders in addition to the commonly understood external community stakeholders. Broadening the category of potential stakeholders to include city staff enables us to develop strategies that not only facilitate the installation of public artwork but also ensure that the benefits of civic engagement—the development of knowledge, skills, values, and motivation—can accrue to both groups of stakeholders. Moreover, we do not consider civic engagement to be a fixed activity, seeing it instead as a fluid and dynamic process that unfolds over time.

Our approach to civic engagement uniquely positions our public art program within the city government as an instrument that can elevate the quality of life for all Angelinos, fulfilling one of the highest ideals of the public sector.

NOTE

1. Ehrlich, in his preface to Thomas Ehrlich, ed., *Civic Responsibility and Higher Education* (Westport, CT: American Council on Education and Oryx Press, 2000), vi; http://www.ipfw.edu/offices/resp/community_engagement/definition-of-engagement-terms.html.

Index

About the Editors and Contributors

Barbara Benish has been working closely with the United Nations Safe Planet Campaign on Hazardous Chemicals and Wastes, where she is an advisor in arts, education, and outreach. Benish is also involved with the U.S. UN Education Caucus and Transformative Education Forum (TEF). She is currently coauthoring a book with an EU-based social science group on environmental art. Her NGO ArtDialogue works toward building cultural discourse through creativity, research, public engagement, and experiential learning for students at their site in Central Europe: ArtMill.

Nigel Brookes has been an arts management specialist with the City of San Diego Commission for Arts and Culture since 2005, where he performs budget and policy analysis as well as public art project management. He managed the two City of San Diego public artworks mentioned in chapter 9. A native San Diegan, Brookes has been studying, writing about, creating, and showing art his entire life. He earned a master's degree in communication from San Diego State University, with a research and teaching emphasis in symbolism and philosophy of language. His graduate research investigated art making as a specialized form of communication, premised on the idea that art makers are creating unique languages to represent unique experiences. As founding member of the San Diego–based Ancient Gallery artist collective, his current interests combine medieval aesthetics with early twentieth-century surrealism through the use of assemblage sculpture in the service of site-specific black light installations and as a location for performing myth, ritual, and adult puppetry. His most recent installation was for the 2014 San Diego Fringe Festival. He lives with his wife, Margy, approximately two miles from the Fairmount Avenue Corridor.

Sherri Brueggemann is the public art urban enhancement program manager for the City of Albuquerque, Cultural Services Department. She holds a bachelor's of university studies from the University of New Mexico (UNM), with an emphasis in public art management, and a master's from UNM's School of Public Administration, with an emphasis in cultural policy evaluation. Sherri was a founding member of the Americans for the Arts Public Art Network and served on the PAN Council from 2000 to 2002. She has been a Lecturer at UNM's College of Fine Arts since 2008 and has served as a board member for numerous arts, cultural, and civic nonprofit organizations in the Southwest, including the New Mexico Route 66 Association and the Albuquerque Arts Alliance and 516 Arts. She helped spearhead the Albuquerque/Bernalillo County Arts and Cultural Industries Economic Impact Study, the ABQ Cultural Count Task Force, and the New Mexico MainStreet Downtown Arts and Cultural District. She is a current member of the board of directors of New Mexico Lawyers for the Arts.

Carrie Brown previously managed public art projects for the Los Angeles County Arts Commission, the cities of Mesa and Glendale (Arizona), and Valley Metro Rail. Carrie received a BFA in photography from Arizona State University and currently serves as chair of Texas Public Art Administrators and on the board of the Austin chapter of Emerging Arts Leaders.

Jessica L. Deshazo is an assistant professor at California State University, Los Angeles, in the Department of Political Science. Her area of expertise includes public art and cultural arts management, sources management, and environmental policy.

Janeil Engelstad is founding director of MAP—Make Art with Purpose, an organization and virtual resource center for creative projects that shape and transform the world in positive ways. She has been working with SPARC via a creative partnership of mutual support. Englestad is an affiliate artist at the Social Practice Art Research Center. MAP's initiatives include an interactive, open-source website, projects and exhibitions, and public programs that engage communities and promote social practice throughout the world. Engelstad's process involves embedding herself in communities; deep listening; extensive research; and building coalitions between community members, arts institutions, universities, government agencies, NGOs, and others. These projects often create a place for individuals and groups who do not have access to art-making opportunities or a voice in society to express their identities, experiences, and points of view. Engelstad was named a 2014 Dallas Mastermind for the lasting impact that this project has had in the greater Dallas Fort Worth community. Several of the projects that Engelstad has coproduced through MAP were featured in her 2014 TEDx SMU talk, "Public Art: from Individual Expression to Community Transformation." Engelstad has taught and lectured at universities throughout North America and Europe. In 2006 she was a Fulbright Scholar at the Academy of Fine Arts and Design in Bratislava, Slovak Republic, and she writes critical reviews for the online publication *Eutopia*.

Felicia Filer is the public art director for the City of Los Angeles Department of Cultural Affairs. She has overseen the commission and fulfillment of over 170 permanent public art projects throughout the city, six site-specific dance performances, and thirty temporary public art projects in nontraditional spaces. Previously Filer worked as a senior management consultant and loan fund manager for ARTS, Inc., a Los Angeles nonprofit arts management consulting organization. A native of Los Angeles, she earned a BS in economics from the University of California, Santa Cruz, and an MBA in finance and marketing from the Peter F. Drucker and Masatoshi Ito Graduate School of Management, Claremont Graduate University. Filer's professional interests include designing systems to facilitate governmental support of innovative models of public art.

Anita Glesta is an artist whose work encompasses numerous artistic approaches, from object making to time-based installation sculpture and digital works, including the creation of public mediascapes and actual landscapes. Major public art projects include a permanent outdoor integrated landscape sculpture for the Federal Census Bureau Headquarters (Suitland, Maryland), and *GERNIKA/GUERNICA*, a multimedia installation first exhibited as under the auspices of the Lower Manhattan Cultural Council and White Box in New York City in 2007 and since featured at the MOCAK (Krakow) and the Arthur M. Sackler Museum of Art and Archaeology (Beijing) in 2012 and 2013. Her upcoming project, *WATERSHED*, a public art/public space mediascape, will be projected on the face of the National Theater in London as part of the Totally Thames River Festival in September 2015. Glesta has been the recipient of numerous grants and awards, including the Pollack/Krasner Foundation Fellowship, the NYSCA New Media Technologies Grant, the NYFA Fellowship for the Arts in Environmental Structures, the Puffin Grant, and an Australia Council Grant. She created and taught the Public Art Residency Program, "Reconfiguring Site," at the School of Visual Arts, New York City, from 2006 through 2013. Examples of Glesta's past works can be found at anitagesta.com.

Jean Graham has managed public art projects in Austin since 2000 after ten years of organizing and curating exhibitions for the Austin Museum of Art. She has an MFA from the University of Michigan and a background as an exhibiting visual artist and art director of neighborhood projects.

Dee Hibbert-Jones, associate professor of art and digital art new media at the University of California, Santa Cruz (UCSC), is founder/cochair of the Social Practice Research Center (SPARC) at UCSC, a research center engendering creative responses to social and environmental concerns. Her research looks at the changing nature of public and private spheres, social connectedness, affect, memory, and politics. She creates public art and participatory practice, films, videos, and interactive projects that explore power, politics, and emotions: how people manage and who gets heard. Her work unpacks notions of "otherness," issues of criminal justice and civic responsibility. Dee Hibbert-Jones has produced large-scale collaborative commissions for the National Parks Service, the British Lottery with FRED UK, the Goldman Foundation, and the Packard Foundation in collaboration with public, community, and private agencies. She has screened and exhibited her work in Europe, Israel, Japan, and the United States in museums and international festivals such as Art in General (New York City); Tokyo Zokei University Museum, (Japan); the Israeli Center for Digital Art; and international film festivals in the United States, Canada, Japan, Israel, Germany, Italy, Finland, Poland, Croatia, and others. She has been awarded grants from the National Endowment for the Arts, the Creative Work Fund, the European Cultural Council, Cal Humanities (a partner of the NEH), and the San Francisco Individual Artist's Grant, among others. Her current work is a short (thirty-two-minute) animated documentary, *Last Day of Freedom*, which explores the crisis in our criminal justice system through the stories of families with a relative on death row and was awarded Best Short at the Full Frame Documentary Film Festival (2015)—Academy Award (Oscar) qualifying; the Film Maker Award from the Center for Documentary Studies (Duke University, 2015); and the Justice for All Award at the (In)Justice Film Festival, Chicago (2015).

Donna Isaac holds a master's degree in art history and a master's degree in planning. She has been director of Scottsdale Public Art since 2013 and has worked in public art for nearly a decade. Prior to that, Donna Isaac focused on cross-cultural communication and worked in public process both nationally and internationally on cross-cultural facilitation and consensus building. She has brought this expertise to her work in public art and engaging community with artists who look at interactive and social practice measures. In her work with Scottsdale Public Art, Isaac has overseen the development of Canal Convergence, an annual event that engages the downtown waterfront with a series of art installations both in the canal and throughout the area. With this particular event and in building temporary installations as a critical programming area for Scottsdale Public Art, Isaac has helped to bridge traditional and new models for funding while recognizing the value of public art to economic development and tourism.

Mary Allman-Koernig was appointed to the position of public art coordinator for the City of Aurora, Colorado, in July 2012. She graduated with high honors from Michigan State University with a BA in the history of art and a master's of art in teaching from the George Washington University, with an emphasis in informal learning. She has had a varied career in arts and history-related fields spanning over twenty-five years and seven states.

Sue Lambe is a registered landscape architect in Maine and Texas and spent much of her career as a consulting landscape architect to the public sector in Maine, working at the intersection of landscape, place making, art, and ecology. She consults nationally on design, public art, and planning.

Zachary A. Smith is a Regents' Professor at Northern Arizona University. He received his BA from California State University, Fullerton, and his MA and PhD from the University of California, Santa Barbara. He has taught at Northern Arizona University; the Hilo branch of the University of Hawaii; Ohio University; and the University of California, Santa Barbara, and served as the Wayne Aspinall visiting professor of political science, public affairs, and history at Mesa State College. A consultant both nationally and internationally, Smith is the author or editor of over twenty books and many articles on policy and administration. Currently, Smith teaches in the public policy PhD program in the Department of Politics and International Affairs at Northern Arizona University in Flagstaff.

Robyn Vegas resides in Broward County, Florida, where she is the current program coordinator for Business for the Arts of Broward (BFA), an innovative nonprofit organization that brings business leaders together to advocate for arts and culture on behalf of other arts programs. She formerly was the cultural arts coordinator for the City of Pembroke Pines, where she promoted visual arts, theater, and music programs and spearheaded the Studio 18 artists work space/gallery as well as other innovative programing. She is also an exhibiting fine artist originally from south of New Orleans, Louisiana.

Meghan Wells has an MA in museum science from Texas Tech University and has served as the administrator of the Austin AIPP Program since 2010 and coordinator from 2004 to 2010. In her tenure, the program has grown to include temporary public art, streetscape-integrated artwork, public-private partnerships, and multimillion-dollar artwork commissions.

K. M. Williamson, PhD, is an applied social ecologist and founding director of the Public Art in Public Places Project. She has served as consultant with Urban Public Realm Consulting since 2007, specializing in public space planning, design, and development. She served six years as architectural commissioner and currently serves as planning commissioner for the City of Claremont, California.